THANKS FOR THE TEA, MRS BROWNE

My Life With Noel

D1434121

THANKS FOR THE TEA, MRS BROWNE

My Life With Noel

Phyllis Browne

New Island Books
Dublin

THANKS FOR THE TEA, MRS BROWNE
First published October 1998 by
New Island Books
2 Brookside
Dundrum Road
Dublin 14
Ireland

Reprinted November 1998

British Library Cataloguing in Publication Data
A catalogue record for this book is available from the British
Library

ISBN 1 874597 85 5

**New Island Books receives financial assistance from The Arts
Council (An Chomhairle Ealaíon), Dublin, Ireland.**

Grant-aided by the
Arts Council

Cover design: Slick Fish design, Dublin
Typesetting: New Island Books
Printed in Ireland by Colour Books, Ltd.

Contents

Dedicated to Noel
in death as in life.

Introduction

Coming away, after a long afternoon in their white-washed cottage, about a year before Noel Browne died, a colleague and I talked about Noel and his wife Phyllis, about the political and the personal. They had moved house twenty-six times, Phyllis reckoned, and now they had come to rest in the cottage which they had slowly renovated over many years. Whitewashed outside, stone and wood inside, thatched roof; impossibly high-ceilinged, small windows, chairs turned to the fire; a very pretty place, and very much shaped by the personalities of the two who shared it. Marx and Lenin on the wall, and a gentle statue of Italian marble, showing a mother and child.

After leaving (and, yes, we thanked Phyllis for the scones and the tea), my colleague and I agreed about how lucky they were, in those final years, to still have a relationship which — there's no other word for it — glowed. As Noel talked about past conflicts Phyllis sometimes mocked him, making a chattering gesture with one hand, and he smiled back at her. Mock she might, but she listened intently to his every word, as though he was someone she had recently met and she was thinking he was something special and maybe she ought to take an interest in him.

With this book, Phyllis has told her own story, and the personal story of the partnership between herself and

Noel. It is a companion piece to his book, *Against the Tide*, in much the same way as they were companions in their long personal and political lives together. It recalls the formal, restrained and often cold family life from which Phyllis emerged. Here and there we come across casual incidents which point up the routine sectarianism and inwardness of a time too easily lauded as the good old days, the rare oul' times. In her simple story of a young friend, Barry, a student with a promising life ahead of him, we glimpse the personal effects of TB, the dreaded disease, the ravaged communities. The book is also in places delightfully romantic. And, in the sadness which suffuses the end, it reminds us that although Noel Browne lived a long and rewarding life, there is no "good age" at which to die, not when the sadness left behind is unbearable.

The value of an introduction to this book can only be in setting the context for Phyllis' personal story, for those for whom the battles of long ago are blurred, and for those born more recently for whom that Ireland is as distant as the Victorian era.

Noel Browne was born a year before the 1916 Rising. His early years dictated how he would live the rest of his life. He was one of eight children and by the time he was twelve, both his parents and a brother and sister had been struck down by TB. His family shattered, Browne would himself barely survive the disease.

What novelist would be so unrealistic as to invent for such a penniless boy the accident by which he would be taken up by a generous and wealthy family and given the best education that money could buy? And even if Jeffrey Archer had been foolish enough to invent such a tale, would he dare give the family that rescued Noel Browne the name Chance? Nevertheless, it was the family of Sir Arthur Chance that befriended Noel. And who would be daft enough to imagine that same boy graduating as a doctor and setting himself the task of combating TB?

That someone with that history should find himself approached to stand for the Dáil, that a chance political wave should throw his small party into coalition in government, that he should immediately become Minister for Health with a brief to fight TB, makes the story too improbable even for someone in the fairytale business. For Browne, the fight against TB was both a medical and a political campaign.

Whatever the bishops said about him Noel Browne would never lose the respect and affection of his people. Countless families, including my own, owed him a life saved and were aware of his importance in our lives.

He also, almost incidentally, set up the blood transfusion service and organised an astonishing hospital building programme. Then, job done, he considered quitting politics, going back to medicine. Instead, he took up a Fianna Fáil proposal to take care of the health of mothers and their newborn. The doctors and the bishops decided this must be stopped. The doctors saw a threat to their income; the bishops were (and today it is quite bemusing to recall) ideologically opposed to the state providing free health care for all mothers and children. They mounted a vicious covert campaign; Browne's government colleagues had no stomach for taking on the bishops; Browne's party leader, Sean McBride, bowed the knee to Maynooth; Browne was easily out-manoeuvred by superior forces.

The mother and child provisions would later be seen as the unremarkable measures they were. It was never about the health of citizens, rather it was about the power of the elites. In imposing its will on the government, the Catholic hierarchy won a battle; by crushing Noel Browne's ministerial career, and by provoking him into making public the private correspondence about the issue, they inadvertently brought their power games into public view. The political clout of the hierarchy would never be the same again.

Had Noel Browne bowed and scraped and accepted the right of interest groups to re-write legislation along lines that suited them, we would never have discovered just how the secret power games worked. Taoiseach John A Costello: "All this matter was intended to be private and to be adjusted behind closed doors...The public never ought to have become aware of the matter."

Browne paid the price; three years a minister, thirty years on the backbenches. Yet in those three years Browne played a central role in two of the major achievements of his time: the elimination of TB and the exposure of the relationship between the Catholic bishops and the politicians. Reckless impetus, some said: if he had played a more careful, pragmatic hand, recognising that politics is the art of the possible, he would have had a long ministerial career. But it was the pragmatists who gave us decades of careful, prudent, sterile inertia. In later years they gave him the old flawed-hero routine ("difficult", "maverick"), a well-practised way of shifting emphasis from the political balance of forces to the character of the protagonists. But Noel Browne will remain a uniquely admirable figure in twentieth-century Ireland. He got in, did the job, retained a sense of proportion, poked an accusing finger at the self-important, never forgot who he was, and paid the price. In an age of professional politicians who can come down with equal passion on either side of any argument, Noel Browne was a one-off.

Noel Browne and Phyllis Harrison married in 1944. You'll have him, a doctor told her, for no more than six months. Over fifty years later she would smile at the memory. They shared views on most things political. If anything, said Noel, Phyllis' grasp of radical politics was more certain than his own. When speaking of his political life he usually used the term "we", meaning himself and Phyllis. Her role was never public, but they were partners: we did this, we did that, we supported this and we opposed the other. There was a pair of them in it. "We never", he told me, "really felt that there was any other purpose in life except this business of making some kind of contribution to an evolving society. We wouldn't change it for anything, either, even though it was hard times."

In his early fifties, having lost his ministerial job and upset the medical profession, Noel Browne found himself almost unemployable as a doctor, shut out from all but the most menial jobs. He went back to school and spent several years qualifying as a psychiatrist. The extraordinary circumstances of his early life had left him with an almost pathological need to contribute in whatever way possible to the collective good.

For thirty years, in concert with his political and personal partner, Phyllis, he stalked the periphery of the political arena, grouchy and bitter, compassionate and provocative. He added his weight to many causes, from gay rights to the defeat of corporal punishment in schools. He accumulated no wealth; no business interests queued up to fill his pockets; he left one very moving and illuminating book behind, but no political writings or structure that promotes his beliefs. By the measure applied to political careerists for whom the job exists for its own sake, not for what can be done with it, he was a loser. But a beautiful loser who set standards that today's political winners couldn't even attempt to meet.

To some he would always be that impossible man with any number of bees in his bonnet; that non-team player. To others of us he was a singular politician who raged against the afflictions which plagued his people, and who — through chance, determination and courage — managed to do something about them. And if he wasn't as sly, as pragmatic, as efficient in his plotting as many a professional politician, so be it.

At the end he came to live out his final years in the cottage he loved, on the land he loved, with the woman with whom he had seen half-a-century of wonderful victories and souring defeats. Together they shared the memories of that long partnership, the personal and the political. Alone now, Phyllis has recorded, as Noel once urged her to do, her own story. Telling a worthwhile story in its own right, her book also provides another perspective on two complementary lives committed to "this business of making some kind of contribution to an evolving society".

Gene Kerrigan, September 1998.

"It is an ever fixed mark,
That looks on tempests, but is
never shaken."

"Love alters not with his brief
hours and weeks,
But bears it out even to the
edge of doom."

from Sonnet CXVI
William Shakespeare

Foreword

Since the death of my Noel I have been living by myself, more or less in silence, speaking to very few people, apart from an occasional telephone chat, or meeting with my good neighbours in the boreen. Hence, the writing of my story was, for many months, known only to myself and done for therapeutic reasons alone — certainly with no thought of it ever reaching a printing press.

One afternoon our friend of some years, Bill Long, a writer himself, called to visit. Noticing that my table was strewn with used writing paper, he enquired as to what I was doing. I told him, and it was he who started the ball rolling, by suggesting that as he thought my life with Noel was a little unusual it might interest his own publisher, Edwin Higel of New Island Books. "Send it," he encouragingly said.

So that is what I did, with some anxiety (for after all, I am a complete novice in the art). On reading the short piece, Edwin kindly told me that he was interested, and encouraged me to continue.

So, firstly, I thank Bill Long and Edwin Higel for their support, their belief in my ability to write my story, and their much-needed encouragement. So many times I asked Edwin in a doubting voice: "Do you really think I can do it?" He always smilingly assured me that I could!

To Ann Marie, who, with patience, care and attention, typed many thousands of words for me, I am really grateful. Thanks to my ever-attentive grandson Glyn and his wife Pam, watchful always for my every need; my beloved daughters Ruth and Sue; their children, Nena, Glyn, Cormac, and Ruairi; all of whom continue to show concern in the nicest possible and practical ways — for they too greatly miss the one we loved so much, my Noel. I really appreciate their efforts, for as with all young people, they are busy working and studying.

Finally, I know no words with which I can adequately thank Ciara Considine of New Island Books for her helpful interest. She worked so hard on my behalf, thought so deeply over every little problem. It was a new and pleasant experience for me to meet such unselfishness, coupled with her delightful sense of humour, in assisting me with my book.

Thanks for the Tea, Mrs Browne is a simply written story, recording some of the domestic highlights in the lives of two complicated persons who were inextricably linked together for more than sixty years.

As far back as 1991, Noel handed me a large empty copybook — in which, inside the cover, he had written '*Mo scéal fhéin*, Phyllis Harrison' — asking me to write my own story. When, in 1997, we were parted forever, I thought I would try to do so, even though I had little experience in writing. As it was, six years had already gone by before I found time to do as he wished. The reason for this delay is simple. Those last six years of his life passed so busily, with so many welcome visitors calling — journalists, authors, photographers, students — trying to clear their minds about his mind.

On these occasions, Noel, who was proud of my cooking, would suggest tea. I have a foolproof recipe for scones, so these I always made there and then: hot, with raisins and smothered with melting butter, after sandwiches to start. It must be sixty years ago since I first made these scones, so easy to make, so quick to cook. I just have to be always sure I have the ingredients in the cupboard.

A young boy, a friend of our daughters when they were ten or twelve years of age, came to play with them every Saturday afternoon. When saying his polite 'goodbyes', he never failed to add "And thanks for the tea Mrs Browne". Many visitors through the years said the same, though not always as sweetly.

While I was pleased that they appreciated my cooking, their remarks made me feel as though that was my function, and no other. Also, I was curiously amused, as well as appreciative, of a number of old friends who wrote to me after Noel passed away, mentioning in their letters how they enjoyed the 'delicious scones', 'the pancakes', 'the home-made icecream' which they were offered on their visits.

But I wondered: did they think I was good for something more useful, or nothing else but cooking? Sometimes I was tempted to tell them that most of the paintings in the room were my work, the chairs had been upholstered by me, the patchwork and embroidery was mine, as well as various other accomplishments. It was with these thoughts in mind that I agreed to the quirky title for this book.

Nonetheless, I have always enjoyed welcoming the many visitors who called throughout the years. So, to all those who were so kind to my Noel, all his ex-patients whom he lovingly cared for during his life, and to all who might find themselves in this district (or even, perhaps, a politician), I'll gladly offer you tea and hot scones.

And for any reader who might wish to try my foolproof recipe for scones, here it is:

Mrs Browne's Scones

Preheat oven to 220°.

Mix two cupfuls of self-raising flour, one to one-and-a-half cupfuls of sugar, and two ounces of margarine in a bowl until they have the consistency of breadcrumbs. Add an egg, and stir all together. If the mixture seems a little stiff, add a drop of milk. Finally, if desired, add a cupful of raisins. Roll this mixture onto a floured board, and cut into scone shapes. This makes about twelve scones. Cook for ten to twelve minutes. Cover with a damp cloth to keep them soft.

Early Days

It was made clear to me early in my young mind that, like an uninvited guest who would not go home, I was not a welcome member of our family, but an unwanted addition to an already too large household — an added burden to our middle-class family, which was always having to watch the pennies.

Possibly the most emotional, even exciting experience in a woman's life is giving birth, but, after ten years of marriage and the bearing of three sons, Cecil, Frank and Brian, my mother had all she wanted and more. But, to her consternation no doubt, along came a second family, after twelve years: of two daughters, Evelyn, then myself in 1920 and finally my younger brother Roderic. The first three sons were what she considered 'a credit to her'. But the second three children were simply a cross she had to bear. She had had enough, and, young as I was, I felt it.

In a Victorian three-storey-house, with only five bedrooms, the household had to be run more as an institution than a home. With my parents, six children of varying ages, plus an orphaned cousin and his friend who wished to study in Trinity, there were ten people altogether, and a great deal of work for my mother, by this time almost middle-aged. She had no experience whatever of housekeeping before marrying at eighteen years of age, having been brought up in the usual Victorian ignorance of her class concerning such matters. Even if not greatly happy within her own family, she had no domestic worries and was comfortable and secure, for her own mother had plenty of domestic help.

It is the common desire of all of us to be loved and taken care of, so when my father, a gentle good man, proposed to her, she no doubt believed that her future would continue as it had in her own family, comfortable and without sordid financial worries. But then the unexpected happened, the experience of childbearing, a miracle about which she was totally ignorant. On the birth of my own first daughter she told me that she had never wished for another child after her first-born, she found the experience so traumatic. That insensitive remark confirmed my feelings of unwantedness.

Brought up by a domineering Welsh-born mother, and an uninterested father, she was one of a family of six or seven children. Marriage, she thought, would give her freedom and status, so she was quite happy to leave her Victorian cage. Poor lady, she just entered another cage, of a different sort, far more disappointing than she could have imagined. Even though my father loved her dearly, and did all he could to help her in every way, marriage was no liberation for her. A hard life and little joy would be her future lot, as she soon discovered. So, with a heavy heart, and who could blame her, she returned unhappily to her kitchen chores. The helpful machines made possible by electricity had not yet arrived, so lighting and cooking were by gas, and a large black range, requiring many buckets of coal a day, roared away in the kitchen, heating pots and pans of all sizes. What thoughts of self-pity my mother must have had, though she struggled on, as mothers do, accepting with fortitude her 'second family' and the extra work her new situation demanded. Once again she was carrying buckets of coal from the outside yard, bed-making, cooking, and dusting endlessly everyday. How could she bother, indeed how could she find the energy or time to spare to 'mother' her three small children, listen to their chatter, tell them stories, or play simple games with them? Never once did she take us upon her lap to hug us, or put us to bed with a goodnight kiss. She had no time whatever, nor, I suspect, inclination, to show any interest in us, never mind show love towards us, possibly because she felt none.

Extroverted, quick-minded and clever, as I later realised, my mother, had she not married, might have had a satisfying life running a business, not an acceptable role for a woman in those days. She had a talent by which she could create original smart clothes, dresses, coats and hats. Sitting by the fire in the evenings her hands were seldom without clicking needles, ceaselessly knitting, embroidering, indeed anything which would keep her nerves in order, and help her to feel less frustrated or angry with her lot. Or so I thought, though I know she got some satisfaction also with her creations in wool and threads, talents which incidentally taught me a lot which became useful to me in later years.

My gentle father, on the other hand, would sit quietly in his comfortable chair, reading his daily paper, pondering over his crossword puzzle, perfectly content to think and rest, perhaps read a few psalms, and, if necessary, help me with my school work. A couple less matched would be hard to find, but the fact that my father was so gentle, so sensitive, thoughtful of others and, above all, patient beyond belief, kept them together. Theirs was a typical Victorian-style marriage of their time; they had not a lot in common, but, most importantly in those days, both were of the Protestant faith, and of similar social background, more or less. Considering my father's insecure, difficult childhood, I have wondered how his personality remained so pleasant. Born in a little town, Cloyne, in Co Cork, sometime in the 1890s, he was one of a large family of six boys and one girl, whose father lived the precarious life of a 'journeyman musician', always on the move from one of Ireland's big houses to another, entertaining the gentry's guests at their musical evenings with his piano playing and singing. If he heard of a Church needing an organist and choirmaster, even temporarily, he was willing to travel any distance to fill the vacancy, presumably by horse and carriage.

It was while my grandfather was on one of these journeys that he called into a Post Office in a small town in the Midlands. He immediately fell in love with the young lady working there, and in due course married her. Little is known by my family of the backgrounds of either of this couple, except that my grandfather had come to Ireland from Yorkshire and Bourke was the surname of the lady he married. My father never spoke of his young life to me: perhaps it was too painful for him to look back upon. With his father's unsettled way of life and the birth of so many children, life for his mother, my grandmother, must have been especially difficult, trudging from one town to another, from one church or cathedral to another. It was while his parents were in Cloyne, Co Cork, where my grandfather was serving as organist at Cloyne Cathedral, that my father was born.

My grandmother seems to have been a lady of strong character. She certainly looks very stern in an old photograph we used to have in my own home. Anyway, she decided, when it came to having six or seven children, that she could not put up with her journeyings any longer. The children's education, in particular, must have been one of her greatest worries: there was not a great difference between the itinerants' children and hers, as far as schooling was concerned.

With the help of the Masonic Order, I believe, and her own courage, she came to Dublin to settle down and have the children educated as best she could. How her husband fared I do not know, though I expect he continued his lifestyle for as long as he could. I do know that he ended his life by himself, living in a Salvation Army Hostel in Dublin, and that he was seen at any musical event at which my own brother Frank, was by then playing, but he kept to himself, which was sad.

Being of the Protestant faith was a help to my grandmother for, because of the musicianship of most of her boys, Christchurch Cathedral accepted them as choristers, which gave them free education. This love of music was passed on to the next generation in time, as each of my four brothers became involved with music-making of different types. Brian got himself through Trinity by playing saxophone and clarinet every night in the Gresham Hotel. How I used to enjoy helping him to get dressed into his formal evening wear of white tie and tails, as they did in those days. I would always see that his shirt and tie had been laundered, collecting them at the "Swastika" laundry on my way home from school. A good shine on his patent leather shoes, and finally a careful run over of his jacket with the clothes brush, before he rushed off, gave me great pleasure, even though all was done in silence.

My next brother, Frank, worked in a bank for a short time, but was dismissed when it was discovered that he played the organ in the local cinema. In time he became a serious musician, playing the organ in St Patrick's Cathedral, while studying in Trinity for his Mus. Doc. He emigrated to Canada, and worked his way through many universities in America, before returning to Oxford and later Amsterdam, and eventually being accepted as a well-known ethnomusicologist.

Roderic, my youngest brother, played piano beautifully for dances, as indeed did my eldest brother Cecil, though the latter became an engineer. It is with great joy now that I listen to my granddaughter, Nena, play her flute and piccolo while our daughter Ruth accompanies her on the piano.

Sadly for my father, he had to find employment as soon as possible to help keep his mother and his brothers in some sort of comfort. Without a single complaint he spent his adult life working at the dull job of accountancy, keeping the Railway Company's books in order. He would have much preferred to study music, for he had a splendid bass voice. But he got pleasure in other ways, for he loved nature, flowers, hedges, walks by the canals or sea, or cricket matches in the Phoenix Park or Trinity College, especially if one of his sons were playing. Otherwise, his days were spent walking to his office in the Broadstone Railway Station from our home on Cabra Road, four times daily through dusty streets, for all the years until he retired.

A tall man, he was handsome, his large brown eyes always calm. He could not have been considered vain, but he was meticulous about his appearance. Without ever bothering my mother he pressed his suits himself, polished his and everybody's shoes to perfection and, on Sundays, wore his special shoes and spats in perfect shape, to match his chamois gloves. A black silk-covered, silver-handled umbrella, completed the 'ensemble'. These special extras, with his best suit, were kept for Sunday wear, when he sang in the church choir. Otherwise an ordinary suit (and always shining shoes!) were worn for his every-day work.

So, neither happy nor unhappy, certainly solitary, I grew up in this busy house — it could not be called a home — of ten souls, never with a feeling that I belonged to this family, but rather as an onlooker, living a private life with thoughts and secrets of my own, generally of a melancholy nature.

Unhappy Memories

One night when I was about four years of age I went to bed, as usual by myself. Noticing a box of matches on the mantelpiece, I reached for them by climbing on a chair. Excited at the prospect of seeing the pretty lights I knew matches could make, I struck a few, happily watching them as they fell down upon my bed, quickly setting my blankets alight. In a horrifying moment the whole bed was in flames and I became very frightened. Hearing my screams, and seeing the flames through the glass of my bedroom door, my eldest brother, who fortunately was passing on the stairs at the time, ran into me, rolled me in blankets, and ran for help to the local doctor. My mother tried to help, but could do little as her hands got quickly burned, and no doubt she was in a state of shock. Eventually the doctor arrived. After a quick look at me he did not hesitate in declaring that, without doubt, nothing could be done for me, as I would not last more than a day or two. Vivid memories of that night are still with me, of watching the flames with fascination, then the pain.

Ignoring the doctor's gloomy remarks, my brother Cecil, who had taught First Aid to the Scouts, insisted on my being removed to hospital. For almost a year I lay there in great pain, for in those days there was nothing but iodine to help the wounds. It was years before the useful present-day medicines were available. Every morning the sound of the rattling trolley of scissors, knives and bandages being pushed along the wooden floor of the corridor towards my ward terrified me, for in a few moments I would be brought down to the theatre to have my leg dressed.

Gradually, miraculously, after a year's treatment, the wounds began to mend, and I started to feel and look more human again, for my hair had been shorn, and I must have looked like a pathetic starved orphan, a pitiful sight.

I have wondered since whether my personality as well as my body was damaged at this time, for I would not speak to anyone, even my family. Nor did I play with toys, or have stories read to me, as children of that age usually enjoyed — indeed needed. After my return home it was many months before I could walk or play with my sister and brother, and I was a long while unable to walk without pain. Left alone, I amused myself quite happily reading, painting and watching passers-by while I sat on the kitchen window-sill.

Another formative experience of my early childhood — which was so repellent to me that I could not talk about it, even to Noel, until about ten years before his death — began one Saturday afternoon, when the family had gone out to enjoy their half-day's holiday, leaving me, then five or six, reading my weekly comic 'The Playbox'. But I was not safe — they had misjudged the nature of my cousin's friend who, when everyone was out of the house, stayed in, and for a purpose, his sordid secret, a secret which ruined my contentment, and perhaps marred my psyche to some extent. I look back on those Saturday afternoons with feelings of horror and helplessness, for there was no one, not even my mother, to whom I could turn to for help. A lonesome child, I could complain to nobody.

There were eleven steps of old and creaking wooden stairs, leading down to our ground floor, where the kitchen was: the very darkest part of the whole house, full of frightening corners and passages to us children. This man knew I was alone in the kitchen. He knew that the house was empty, and I was there ready to be preyed upon. After the first dreadful encounter, I knew what to expect when I heard him stepping with quiet care down the stairs towards me. I knew immediately when he had reached the eleventh and final step, aware then of the frightening ordeal which faced me.

Watching the brass doorknob of the kitchen slowly, silently turning, I held my breath, trying to make myself smaller, and wishing indeed I could become invisible. But there was no escape. In he came towards me, wearing his ugly sneering smile. "May I read your comic to you? Let me help you with the puzzles." I became used to these preliminaries in time, and refused to answer him, hopelessly wishing for someone, anyone who might disturb him, to knock at the side entrance door. Closer and closer he came towards me, taking me down off the window-sill, and sitting me on his uncomfortable knobbly knees for what seemed an age. His unwelcome, unpleasant fondling then began.

How, why was it, that I could tell nobody of my suffering? I hated this man and how he mistreated me, yet I was afraid of telling my secret. Who in the family would have believed me, for this creature sat at table with my parents and big brothers? Nobody in the family would have thought he was anything but a quiet, studious, perfect gentleman. Looking back at my helpless situation, I realise now the importance of a child having a close relationship with their parents, so that help can be asked for when needed. This man's behaviour continued for the years he was studying, but as I got stronger, eight or nine years old, I was able to escape him by hiding and locking doors, until he was forced to give up. This experience made me aware of such dangers when we had our own two daughters years later on — I never, ever, left them open to such a risk.

Childhood Preoccupations

Having learnt of the fact of death at a young age, at Sunday School, I was greatly saddened by the story of the Crucifixion, wondering how on earth a good God could do such a thing to his son. The fear of the same God deciding to carry out a similar punishment to a member of my family, or a good friend, kept me awake worrying through the night. Why wouldn't he, for I had been told we were sinners all?

My granny was the oldest person in the world, I thought, and I believed that one died when reaching eighty or more. This fear of death haunted me for years. The sight of a house with drawn blinds depressed me, as I would feel so sorry for the family weeping inside. It came to the point where I was afraid to return home from school in case our own window blinds were drawn. As I approached our house I would cycle more and more slowly, until finally one awful day the blinds were drawn. Who was dead? Afraid to knock at the door to find out, I sat out of sight on the granite steps for an hour or more until my father arrived home from his office. Amazed to see me in such a state, he brought me into the house, quite empty, and explained to me that it was my granny who had passed away. I had never seen much of her except when she visited occasionally during school lunch hours with a message for my mother. Except for the fact that she gave me and my little brother a three-penny piece when we had delivered the message, we had little to say to her, nor she to us. She was always sitting up in her bed combing her long grey hair until she had it cleverly pinned into a thick bun at the nape of her neck. When my grandmother spent Christmas with us, I would watch her carefully to make sure she was still breathing properly, as I would have been so frightened to see her die.

Getting older did not entirely relieve me of this discomfort with death, and even when my parents died I did not wish to see them laid out. "Go in to see your father," my mother instructed, and I had to pretend to do so. Many years later, however, I would stay with my Noel until he breathed his final breath, hoping that somehow he could be revived, or if not, I could go with him.

Happier Times

But life when young is not all gloom, and the three of us younger children found plenty of simple ways to enjoy ourselves: spinning tops, playing 'shop' in the garden shed, swinging under the old arch. Our garden was quite narrow, but long, and divided into three parts. The first was for the coal shed, and our cousin Alfred's workshop — he was for ever passing his silent life there (he seldom spoke), sharpening knives and scissors, or mending his radios parts. He was very clever with radio and made his own sets; to our delight he allowed us listen to the very early broadcasts from Athlone, the first national broadcasting transmitter, the beginning of Radio Éireann.

A pleasant grassy lawn with flowers was the middle part of the garden, and finally the bottom third through which we dashed when we heard a train puffing and blowing in Broadstone Station. Soon it would be passing the banks at the bottom of our garden, on its way to God knows where. For all we knew perhaps it would go to Australia, but it succeeded in giving us much excitement while we waved special flags for the occasion. The kindly drivers waved back at us, and if our big brother Cecil was on the engine platform, as part of his engineering course, the excitement was even greater.

Family Celebrations

Birthdays, Easter, Christmas, and anniversaries of every kind were celebrated in my home, remarkable occasions for a family who seldom showed any excitement or emotion. A special cake with decorations and candles would be prepared for birthdays; a Bewley's chocolate 'nest' with little furry chicks in it and pretty decorations around the edge of coloured sugar flowers for Easter, both always served up on our breakfast plates. The weeks before Christmas were full of pleasant anticipation. Preparation would start in early November, when my mother began stoning dozens of muscatels; her own orange and lemon peel would be soaked in sugar syrup for days, before being cut into small pieces for the cake. Nuts were shelled and chopped by hand, and dozens of cherries stoned and likewise chopped. Lastly, charms of three-penny pieces were added to the pudding mixture before it was set into a ball of muslin and put into a large pot to boil for many hours.

Noel would love to hear me tell of our family occasions, and would talk of his mother's attempt to produce her Christmas pudding, which, although a perfect ball inside its muslin, when taken out of the pot, collapsed into a perfectly flat pudding when placed on a serving plate! He disliked the season, and even became morose until New Year's Day came around. Memories of long ago, when his parents, brother and sister were together, flooded his mind at this time: they were together and happy, even though Santa Claus often had only a pair of socks for them. Truth to tell, I was probably no happier than Noel, for, except on Christmas Eve, I disliked when the real celebrations started, as my mother's family of five or six sisters, their husbands and children always came to our house for the evening.

Religious duties came first on Christmas Eve, when we would attend morning service in our local parish church. Carols were sung with great joy by the choir, to organ accompaniment. But one thing troubled me through the service. The organ worked by air being blown into the pipes by a young man, who, standing at the side of the organist, lifted a long handle up and down, without any particular timing. I spent worried months watching this helper, afraid he would forget to use the handle, and leave the organ notes silent. In the afternoon, I looked forward with special pleasure to a visit to St Patrick's Cathedral for their carol service, for the voices of the young boys, one of them my younger brother Roderic, were so beautiful, and the organ playing so majestic, that I was truly moved.

Before taking the tram home, our father brought us down to Grafton Street to see the bright shops, and have tea in Roberts café at the top of the street. Here a trio of lady musicians played as you entered, and we could choose whatever cakes we wished. It was the only day of the year we had such a treat and I felt that my father and mother enjoyed it.

Next day, after our Christmas dinner and rest, the real celebrations began, as far as my mother was concerned. All her family arrived, a noisy crowd of twenty-five or so. She had spent the afternoon laying out the table with a magnificent collection of buns, cakes, sandwiches, jellies and cream and in the centre an enormous fruit cake with the decorations in place. Our grandmother got pride of place, while we children sat at a separate table, more or less in silence for we hardly knew one another, meeting only at Christmas times. But we knew that after tea we could look forward to the arrival of Santa, who would knock loudly on the front door, wearing a red coat and hat, a large white beard, with a big sack on his back, full of hoped-for surprises.

Tables were cleared, chattering aunts and uncles found comfortable chairs and stayed quiet for a while as the sack was emptied of the gifts, each named and called out by Santa – whom we realised a few years later had been my oldest brother. Needless to say, there were some disappointments as we children opened our parcels, for what child wants socks, gloves, or a woolly hat from Santa? The odd box of sweets saved the day, and the special separate gifts from our own parents helped: a box of paints, a scooter, even a Holy Bible from my father, which I still have with his greeting inside the cover and the date, 1932, inscribed.

The final miserable end to the evening was more carol singing, accompanied by one of my uncles who, much to my dismay, played the piano as though it was an organ – for he played that instrument in a city church – resulting inevitably in more missing notes from my beloved piano. We children had to do a 'turn': Evelyn danced, Roderic sang 'Oh for the wings of a dove', and I played the piano, but nobody listened. Again, every carol in the book was shouted out in their trembling voices, as if the Lord himself would hear them.

All the aunts were big heavy ladies. My mother would instruct us to say goodnight, thank them and kiss them, and I remember my difficulties in doing this, for their large bosoms made it impossible for me to see their faces. With relief I could see that the evening was coming to an end when my grandmother — dressed in her usual long black taffeta skirt, edged with lace and jet beads, her hair pulled back off her stern face into its bun on the back of her neck — stood in the centre of the room, while her daughters and their husbands joined hands and circled her, singing the Welsh anthem, for she was born in Wales.

Soon I could disappear to bed with my new treasures, happy that another Christmas was over. If only Noel had been the boy next door, how much more fun we would have had!

Summer Holidays

Our summer holidays were always spent in Skerries, at that time a pretty, quiet, fishing village, north of the city. After weeks of preparation, deciding what books, toys and clothes we wished to bring with us, we would be collected by a kind cousin who would drive us there in his large open-top motor car. This drive, of about twenty miles, was in itself a great treat, for it was the only time throughout the whole year when we had a journey by car.

My mother would have chosen a suitable cottage for the month, generally thatched, by the seashore, and with a small garden for our play, although, if we wished, we could play in safety for as long as we wanted on the rocks, searching for crabs, and watching the fishing boats coming and going into the little harbour. We could even walk safely to the shops, or the mill, about half-a-mile away, where we would collect hot bread for our tea.

A walk by the seashore brought us to the mill, a real mill by a stream, which we excitedly crossed by stepping-stones. The inviting smell of the hot baked bread hurried us to the ladder where the friendly miller stood, waiting to greet us and be paid. With the loaves in a basket we raced through the fields, a shortcut home, resting for a while in the sweet-smelling meadows and wheat fields, where we tasted a few crumbs, just a few, from the loaves, and picked wild flowers to bring home. How happy childhood memories can stay in your mind for so many years! While resting on the meadows, we could look back at the pretty sight of the mill and the old tall spired church we attended for Service every Sunday morning — in our best clothes of course. These were indeed happy, carefree days, ending with the sound of waves breaking on the shore, lulling us to sleep with sea music.

Everyone knew almost everyone else in Skerries, for the same families holidayed there year after year, so we were all good friends, enjoying ourselves together, swimming and diving in the little harbour during the days, picnicking on the sands in the evenings, or going to the 'seaside concert party' in the hall, where every night the same performance was given. I will always remember that the first compliment I was ever paid, as a young teenager, was given to me in Skerries. It was during one of our picnics. Compared to the other girls in the party I felt inexperienced and unsophisticated. Sitting in a circle the boys were asked to "smile at the wittiest, kneel to the prettiest, kiss the girl you love the best"! The boys duly paid their respects, according to their taste. Coming to my turn I nervously waited — would any of the boys consider me to be pretty or witty? To my amazement one of the boys quietly said, "Phyllis is all three to me!" and pecked my cheek, to everyone's cheers! I wonder does he still remember this gallant gesture? He's probably happily married since — I hope so — and our game quite forgotten by him.

It was in Skerries, also, a few years later after our game on the dunes, that I met Barry, with whom I became close friends. He was a gentle boy and we had much in common. He lived quite near us in Dublin, so that I met him often in the tram while he was going to University to study engineering, and I was going to school. He lived with his sisters and widowed father, who, if I called to Barry's sisters, would always open the door to me, but never spoke a word. Perhaps he was in perpetual mourning for his dead wife, for his face always wore a very sad look.

Barry was a serious student in UCD and seemed to live a quiet studious life. Nevertheless he was laid low with tuberculosis. Although he was five or six years older than I, Barry seemed to rely on me for any help which would make him feel better, letting me know when he wished me to call to him by sending his sister with a note to me at home. After my visit he would appear to be more cheerful for some days, according to his sister, but he never did recover, for she called one day to ask me to visit him in the Hospice. I really dreaded this idea, knowing what it meant — Barry was dying — and I would find it difficult to handle the situation.

However, I crossed the city, slowly walking to the Hospice as though my lack of speed would put off the arrival. I found Barry obviously glad to see me, even smiling. I sat beside him, while he chatted as best he could with his tired lungs, and I tried to keep him interested with gossip of our mutual friends. After a while I thought I should leave him, as a great tiredness seemed to have fallen upon him. As I moved to go, thinking he was sleeping, to my total amazement he spoke. "Promise to marry me when I get better," he said.

What could I say to a dying man? It was a ludicrous notion. To smile and nod to him was all I could bring myself to do. He died next day, and I cried.

Growing Up a Little

The three of us younger children were growing up and though Skerries holidays were over for good, there were still a few pleasures to be had. These especially included Sally, a typical Dublin black-shawled lady, who pushed her three-wheeled wicker basket along our road on Saturday afternoons, while she called out all the while, "Any old jam jars". Old and worn by weather and worry, she never failed to wearily trudge along, her basket filled with a selection of pretty coloured beads, threads, paints and all sorts of little treasures. We would rush to the pantry to collect as many jars as we could carry and patiently wait until she reached our gate. With Sally happily watching, beaming her toothless smile kindly at us, we made our choices, mine quickly and secretly hidden in my special old handbag which my mother had thrown out. I went through this bag every night before going to sleep, admiring my collection, old and new.

Sally was very special, for she made such a pretty sight. On one side of her basket handle was tied an enormous black net, filled with large balloons of every colour: just one more jam jar bought you one. Watching her as she trundled up the hilly road, I was always anxious for her, especially on a windy day. What if the wind might catch her net of balloons, and carry it up to the clouds?

On summer days we would pack a picnic and walk to the Phoenix Park, or Finglas Woods, which at that time seemed to me to be a carpet of bluebells, primroses, or whatever other flower was in season, except in autumn, when all was dying and falling, showering the ground with dry dead crackling leaves, fun to shuffle into piles and roll about in. Our "picnic" was bread and butter, sandwiched with greengage jam, always greengage jam, but we were always hungry and glad of it.

Winter brought the gaslighter for the street lamps, whom we watched with awe as he smartly walked the long distance to the end of the road, criss-crossing to the lamp-posts on each side. With his long pole he reached to the glass of the lampshades, pushed it gently upwards, then, as though the pole were a long match stick, he magically gave the lamp a butter-yellow light. On and on the poor man walked, no matter what the weather.

Our childhood and its pleasures were gradually passing, but there was one large distasteful part of our young years which we were pleased to leave behind us, and that was the presence of Kathleen, the 'nurse' whom my mother employed to look after us. An unpleasant sour lady — no doubt unhappy — she had tormented us for six years. Now we were getting bigger and better-able to look after ourselves, and there was also the question of finding room for her in the house as we moved into bedrooms of our own, and so she left us, without any of us shedding a tear. Her temper frightened us, for if she wished, she could use the leather strap which hung on the kitchen wall by the range, well out of our reach, but not hers. For no good reason she would chase us around the kitchen table with it — fortunately for me, as I was small enough to get under the table and sit on the bench until she cooled down. But as we were brought up separately from the family, having all our meals with her, and no fun whatever unless we made our own, we were understandably glad to see her go.

Unfortunate Others

As I entered my young teenage years, I was still timid and introverted, and problems, even though fairly trivial, made me even more solemn. I had to cross the city to get to my school, The Diocesan School for Girls on Adelaide Road, and would purposefully pass through the back streets of Dublin, the most dreadful slum areas, where the children were barefooted, the small boys dressed in raggy clothes, selling newspapers at cold windy corners; mothers with joyless faces, holding their babies in halls out of the wind and rain, and numerous hungry-looking children running around. These sights saddened me as I passed by, holding my breath as best I could for fear of catching a disease. What a difference, I thought, between the north of the city, where I lived in Cabra Road, and the south, where my school was. I wondered why life was so hard for some, so much easier for others.

We had a spinster aunt who, every Monday evening, visited my mother, her sister, to have a chat and a cup of cocoa. Along with her pet 'pom' dog, she brought a large bundle of Church magazines, and British children's newspapers for us children. There were always unhappy stories in these papers — a father who was a heavy drinker and violent, the mother and children scared of him, and little money for even simple food. I would read these stories before going to sleep, tearfully, every night until the following Monday, when our aunt would ask us questions about them, and give us more to read.

Depressing as the stories were, I suppose I learnt something from them, and indirectly from my aunt. I realised that it was religion plus the interference of the State which kept these poor people down, and dictated their standard of living. Constantly praising the British and blaming ourselves, the Irish, for all our woes, she would say: "There's no such person as a good Catholic." I had to sort this problem out, for there were deprived people in England too, according to her magazines, but it was not easy for me, as the rest of my relations of that generation remained sectarian bigots to the end of their days, making it impossible for me to find anyone in the family who would explain their hatreds and give me answers to my questions.

In school I felt I was being taught the exact opposite of what I myself believed — what I could see as fact with my own eyes. My teachers were of the opinion that those who were unemployed were 'lazy'; "it's their own fault, they don't want to work," they would say. I felt differently, for what human being wishes to live in misery? To leave things as they were was the attitude of my teachers, so my wondering and I were alone as ever.

My only real interest was music — the soul embodied in sound. Since I reached seven years of age I had been taking piano lessons from an excellent teacher, Sheila Rumbolds, who lived near our home. Part of the pleasure of my lessons was just admiring the beauty of this lady, her pink and cream complexion, serene smile, and golden hair which fell in little curls over her forehead. I worked hard to please her for a few happy years, until, sadly, I had to move on, quite loathe to leave her. Due to her, and her patience with my work, I was successful in winning a scholarship to the best pianoforte school in Dublin at that time. I also took violin lessons from a pretty Jewish lady, Posy Shreider, but she left Dublin to join the Hallé Orchestra in Manchester. This life was much more pleasurable than learning algebra or arithmetic, and gave me time to attend concerts and recitals. An English concern used to send famous musicians to Dublin, and I was lucky to hear Kreisler, Horowitz, Jasha Heifitz and many more, for the princely sum of one shilling, given to me by my brother Brian.

Aged about fifteen at this time, I knew I should have still been attending school, but my parents did not appear to take any interest in my future and I could come and go as I wished. Painting and drawing were subjects which I had enjoyed in school, so I went to the Metropolitan College of Art in Kildare Street, in between piano lessons, but found it waste of time. My own fault perhaps, but I could never find the teachers to be interested in giving lessons; pupils I spoke to said they were in their private rooms, doing their own work most of the day. So I left after a few months, disappointed; my formal education, such as it had been, was over at the age of fifteen. Truth to tell, I learnt a lot more about life after I left school. It was a case of bringing myself up, learning by the example of other peoples' lives, constantly listening and watching, noticing the various reasons for the ups-and-downs of life, and learning also to enjoy the good times, and accept the bad. Our experiences when young stay unconsciously at the back of our minds, to form the adult we become, what we believe, and how we look at the world.

Ethnic Cleansing, de Valera Style

At this time, my sister Evelyn, a few years older than I, and far more sensible, decided to start nursing as a career, so she left home for Dr Steevens' Hospital, Dublin, where, I understand, she was considered to be an excellent nurse. My youngest brother, Roderic, a few years younger than I, was sent to a boarding school, King's Hospital in Blackhall Place in Dublin, which has since moved out to a pleasant area near Palmerstown. The Blackhall building was very old, built by King Charles II for the education of poor Protestant boys, an uncomfortable joyless place, reminiscent of Dickens' time, I'm quite sure it is greatly improved since it has been taken over by Dublin Law Society. I would visit Roderic on Saturday afternoons, bringing a parcel of his favourite biscuits and fruit, but I don't think he was at all happy there, except at games, cricket especially, for they had a fine playing field.

Now I was by myself, at home with my parents, or I might as well have been, for my three older brothers were studying and working and seldom at home. I still had no idea of what I wanted to do with my future life. It was a particularly difficult time for Protestant families, especially if they wished to take up employment in Ireland. Now that we were a so-called 'Free State', Church and State were in a great hurry to run the country in a way which pleased them both, taking important powers onto themselves. Mr de Valera, always with the agreement of the Roman Catholic hierarchy, was anxious, indeed determined, to have the country run by as few Protestants as possible. It was difficult for a Protestant to be accepted for a position of any importance, such as doctor, nurse, teacher, or even librarian. Not only was

46

their religion in question, but they were also required to be capable of speaking the Irish language. Excluded from employment for which they had trained and were capable, many Protestants had no option but to emigrate to make a living.

As a result of that, my unfortunate brothers, most of my close relations, and many Protestants unknown to me, were forced to leave their own country, which they all loved, and join what is lately called the 'Diaspora': in other words, to emigrate. Well-educated, and talented, their various abilities were lost to their own country, which greatly needed them to help build up our new Ireland. All of my brothers, while managing to find employment in Ireland upon graduating from college, found their prospects within the given jobs greatly diminished as a result of their background, being both Protestants and Trinity graduates.

This unfortunate state of affairs eventually led to years of dreadful suffering for two of my brothers, who having decided to emigrate to the Far East, Malaya and Singapore, were taken as prisoners of war by the Japanese, during the Second World War. For almost five years they suffered unbelievably cruel treatment. My eldest brother Cecil was by this stage a Civil Engineer, and working for the Colonial Office in Malaya on the construction of the railway line there when he was captured by the Japanese and taken to a work camp on a nearby island, where he was to spend the next five years of his life. Another brother, Brian, was a Professor in Oriental Languages at the University of Singapore when he was taken as prisoner by the Japanese and sent to Changai Jail for four years. As with many other prisoners of war, all of his belongings were taken from him, and he later recalled to me how he looked helplessly onwards as his new car was dumped in the harbour by the Japanese. There was nothing anyone could do to help these men, indeed we were not even sure whether they were alive or dead. When they did return home, they were completely changed personalities, and would never tell us of their dreadful experiences, not even to their parents or wives and children, of those who had managed to escape.

By now, of course, this is past history, the number of Protestants is no longer a threat to the Catholic Church, and Trinity now is, as it always should have been, full to capacity of students from all lands, of all beliefs. It is no longer a 'sin' for those of the Catholic faith to study there without permission from the Catholic Archbishop of Dublin, as it was in the past. Noel himself never did ask permission to attend Trinity; he was not aware of the necessity, having only arrived back in Ireland a short time before enrolling there, after years at school in England.

The Beginning
of My Future

A Tall, Dark-Brown-Eyed Man

Within a few years my brothers qualified for their various professions and emigrated. That left just myself and my parents in the home, once so busy, now silent, each of us brooding over the fate of the missing members, for rumours of a coming war were spreading. My own heart was heavy as I pondered over my own future, for at sixteen I knew not what direction I was going in. One evening, sitting around the fire having our simple supper before going to bed, I watched my parents detachedly, trying to imagine how once they had been young and in love. If long years ago they were full of joyful plans, now all they seemed to have in common were memories and worries about their children. Would this be my future too? I felt dismal, desolate, solitary as ever, and went off to bed.

On my way, as always, I dropped into the piano room to play a favourite piece, most likely a Beethoven Sonata, in the minor key as usual. Lost in my music, I was startled by a ring of the front doorbell. Timidly opening the door, for it was a late hour for visitors. I was relieved to see Michael, whom I had known for years, for he lived almost opposite to us in a fine large house. I asked him in, wondering why he was calling at such an hour, nearly eleven o'clock. I thought that perhaps he was in trouble with his father, the owner of a large well-known public house in the city. When we were younger we greatly feared meeting him as he staggered and shuffled his way home, a hopeless alcoholic. But Michael, the publican's son, was a quiet gentle boy, a little older than myself.

"Would you care to come with me to the Trinity Boat Club dance?" he asked. Of course I accepted with delight, for I loved to dance. Quickly changing into the best finery I could gather, I left home with my parent's permission. I jumped excitedly into Michael's open sports car, not realising that I was, in a way, leaving home for ever, as I was about to begin a new life, a relationship which would last for the next sixty or so years.

The Boat Club building was beside our well-loved River Liffey, on old-fashioned building remindful of those by the Thames, where, in summer time the English university rowing teams can be seen racing. Into the building Michael and I went, quickly mixing with the crowd of students, enjoying themselves to the pleasant dance music of the day. "Like a drink?" asked Michael. As I waited for him on the steps of the clubhouse, a tall dark-brown-eyed, coal-black-haired young man a few years older than I came towards me out of the bar, carrying a glass of beer. His face was slightly familiar to me, and mine to him, so we smiled and spoke a few words.

It was a habit my girlfriends and I had to 'walk' Grafton Street every Saturday morning, and to chat over coffee in the pleasant surroundings of Mitchell's café. I would have seen him then with his other medical student friends, walking dreamily along, looking down at the pathway, taking no notice of his friends or passers-by. How 'detached' he seemed, I had thought to myself. He had intrigued me.

Now, on the third stair outside the bar of the Boat Club, we met face to face. Leaving his beer on the step, this young man of twenty-one, not so 'detached' tonight, but sure of himself, practically carried me to the dance floor. Instinctively a life commitment was silently understood between us. It was as though we had already lived a life together in the past, lost touch, and were happy now to meet up again. With an occasional sit-down to talk on the grassy river bank, we danced together as one until the party was over. I found it difficult to believe that Noel was seriously interested in me, but the next day and the following years happily convinced me he was. As for Michael, from that evening to this, I never saw him again. I just hope he forgave me for my bad manners.

I remember every thing about Noel, as though I had a photograph of him as he looked that evening, his general appearance, his speech, his smile. He wore a well-tailored jacket, then called an 'Oxford' jacket, a cream silk shirt, and suede shoes. Extremely tall, I noticed how long his fingers were, how thin his hands, how large and deep-pool-brown his eyes. He wore his thick black hair long but tidy, and was quietly spoken. As I got to know Noel better, and his ways — so different from my conservative brothers — I realised he had his own taste in clothes, choosing colours and styles just to suit himself, preferably expensive, even having his shoes handmade. Nor was he a 'follower of fashion' in evening wear, never dressing in the standard white tie and tails, but instead in a cream silk shirt, black tie and dinner jacket, saying he preferred to be comfortable. He also greatly disliked having his hair cut.

But on informal occasions and holidays, Noel's taste in clothes changed completely, as I suppose most people's do. What he liked would be a sailor's smock, corduroy slacks, any old shirt, a pullover of the Aran type, which I always knitted for him, and his long unruly hair covered with his navy Breton cap, not a tidy sight at all. On holiday many years ago in Connemara, with our daughters and their friends, we decided to go to Galway city one day. Casually drifting one after the other towards the Spanish Arch area, Noel was accosted by a Garda who asked, "Where are ye camping?" "Out in Connemara," Noel replied, well aware how like an traveller he looked, as indeed we all did. Interestingly, this incident showed us how one's clothes and general appearance are a bad way to judge a person, although we have always been friendly with our local travellers.

Remembering Noel's curious dislike of visiting a hairdresser for a haircut more than three times a year, I recall a very strange coincidence. I had reluctantly gone away with my mother, to the South of England, her idea, I suspected, to take my mind off Noel, of whom she did not entirely approve. How the days dragged by until, back in Dublin, disconsolately strolling near Grafton Street, hoping we would meet by chance, I heard the sound of running feet behind me — it was Noel. Sitting in the window of his hairdresser in Suffolk Street, having one of his few-and-far-between haircuts, he saw me passing by the Trinity College Provost's house. Catching up with me, without a word, we fell into each others' arms. Whenever we passed that location afterwards we always remarked on the *exact* spot, remembering that exciting day of coincidence, and smiling to think of the poor hairdresser whose client jumped out of his chair, with only half of his haircut finished. To the amusement of the hairdresser we had returned immediately to pay him, offering apologies and explanations.

Another extraordinary coincidence happened during the same year. Noel had gone on a sailing holiday with a few friends to Brittany, so I accompanied my brother Brian, who was on leave from his university in Singapore, to Donegal for a few weeks, in his new sports car. We travelled through every part of that beautiful county, visiting little cottages where, generation after generation, families wove and sold their own tweed. Donegal's colours were quite unlike those of any other county I knew. The thick woollen coats of the sheep were saffron coloured, the hedges by the roadside completely covered with the blazing red of fuchsia and the gold of gorse.

But, as lovely as the countryside was, every day I looked forward to our return to Dublin. Throughout the holiday there had been no way Noel and I could communicate. At last the day came to start the journey home. This turned out to be quite an event, for, as we turned a corner on a country road, we met a large lorry carrying rocks, one of which fell off onto our windscreen, forcing us into a deep ditch. After some hours we were lucky to find a few helpful men who towed the car to the nearest town, where we had to stay overnight to have the windscreen replaced.

This delay turned out to be of interest, for if the accident had not happened, neither would the extraordinary coincidence which followed. As Brian and I drove up to our home, having stopped on our way to visit various houses where once our relatives had lived long ago, it was just astonishing to see Noel arrive at the very same moment, in his little black car. I still think that, after a month, without any communication, neither of us having an idea where the other was, it was certainly a remarkable coincidence.

After cheerful greetings and a pleasant meal which my mother already prepared for her favourite son, the conversation turned to cars, Brian's new silver coupe being jokingly compared with Noel's, the tiny beetle-shaped Austin, with no windscreen, no dependable lights, no dependable brakes, and the road visible through parts of the floor.

On a country road near Enniskerry one evening we were stopped by a Garda just before darkness fell. Asked to show his car lights, Noel took a torch out of his pocket, explaining how it was so good that he used it for looking down the throats of patients. To our relief the garda accepted the explanation, but we were not yet quite out of the woods. All the while this conversation was taking place, I was preventing the car from moving on. Having quietly opened my door, I was pushing my foot hard on the ground, holding it back with all my strength. No doubt there were far fewer cars on the roads in those days, far fewer laws for drivers, and far fewer gardaí, which made life much easier for us. But that sort of car was the kind every student drove, if all he had was five pounds to purchase one. Seldom needing petrol, it enabled us to enjoy the freedom we so loved, driving with the wind in our hair, up hills, down dales, wherever we wished, and whenever we were tired of the city, which even in those years, the late Thirties, we considered to be noisy.

So it was that my mind's wondering and wandering in my young years at home became something which I could share with Noel, as my future life of endless interest, pleasure, pain, learning and, I hope, usefulness began. The experiences of each of our very different young lives up to this point would now happily join, keeping us together in a perfect life of understanding and trust, difficult and sad though it would prove at times.

Our First Year

Our first year together was probably the only one during which we were really carefree, walking miles over the Dublin and Wicklow hills, picnicking by their sherry-coloured streams, taking in a play in the old Abbey Theatre, or the Gate, or perhaps a concert in the evenings, new and pleasant experiences which we both enjoyed. Before a reluctant goodnight, we might visit a little Italian restaurant off Dame Street, for a spaghetti meal. If studies needed attending to, we would spend the days reading under the trees in St Stephen's Green, and for refreshment wander down Grafton Street to the Wicklow Hotel for the evening. We were as two skylarks soaring into the heavens every day, with no thoughts whatever of impending doom.

Trinity Days

Then as now students could live in 'rooms' in College. For Noel who had no permanent home of his own, this arrangement was ideal, and for us both it was a perfect base to meet. It would take him only about ten minutes to arrive at his morning lectures on time — out of bed, dress, drink two bottles of milk and quickly run over the old cobblestoned square, to the lecture hall — this was his morning program.

I would call at lunch time, when we would go out to buy our lunch, bringing it back to cook in the little kitchen — eggs to poach, with tinned beans, cheese and fruit, a bottle of Guinness. In summertime we ate pounds of delicious strawberries, cheap to buy then in Findlaters, and, of course, large cartons of cream to cover them.

Trinity is such a beautiful place, whose peaceful atmosphere, though in the centre of the city, must be a help to students in their work. But of course, at that time, in the Thirties and Forties, only the privileged classes were able to avail of its pleasures in learning. My own brothers had to gain scholarships to enter; fortunately for them they were clever and won prizes to help them through their studies. As I was in the grounds almost every day with Noel, many of his friends would ask me what was I studying! There were very few girl students, and any there were came from rich families. My family thought it much more important that the boys were well educated: the girls could always marry!

Maybe because his young life had little regularity, Noel grew up to be unpredictable, a characteristic it took me some time to get used to, myself having been brought up in a fairly strict time-keeping way of life. Noel's family life had been shattered due to death from tuberculosis. His father's death meant losing their home in Athlone, as it had been provided as part of his job. His mother and siblings were forced to move to Ballinrobe, where his mother knew a few people who she hoped could help them, but alas, they had not the money either. Soon after, his mother got ill with tuberculosis, and no doctor would attend to her, nor did any priest call. She decided her only option was to gather all seven children and travel to London where her eldest daughter had a small job and friends would keep them for a short while. Yet a few days after arriving, she herself died. Noel's crippled brother, who also suffered from the disease, was operated upon and died soon after. The eldest sister would be the next victim, but before she died, she managed to get Noel a place in the school in which she worked.

This was to be his saving grace. From there (St Anthony's, Bournemouth), he won a scholarship to Beaumont College Public School where he boarded until he was of school-leaving age. A fellow pupil and friend, Neville Chance, then brought Noel on a visit to Dublin for a holiday, and the Chance family kindly welcomed him, realising he had no home. The four senior members of this large family decided to finance Noel so that he could attend Trinity and study medicine. This was indeed a wonderful stroke of luck for Noel. His good school-friend Neville has sadly passed on, but Noel never forgot his kindness and the kindness of that family. It was when I began to learn about Noel's background that I began also to understand the reasons behind his unsettled and unpredictable nature, as evidenced in the following story.

We would often make an arrangement to meet for a morning coffee and talk, but what would follow was always unexpected. It depended on the weather to a large extent, cinema if it was cold, wet or windy, a walk if the sun was shining. One morning on which I was wearing light summer wear, no jacket and light shoes, Noel suggested a gentle walk through the park. Or so I thought, but something much more out of the ordinary was in his mind, for which of course I was unsuitably dressed. "We'll get a bus first," he said, which pleased me, for I knew nothing of the Dublin suburbs, and looked forward to seeing them.

After an hour's journey by bus, we reached the terminal and started our walk. The first part was easy enough for me to manage, a path by a lake, its water amazingly clear and amber-coloured. After another mile or so a valley of green moss and heather faced us. Through this we walked, all the time in conversation, elated with the beauty of our mountain surroundings. Getting nearer to the sheer side of the valley, I passed no remark, but fought on upwards, uncomplaining, wondering to myself was I being tested like we used to be in the Girl Guides, when trying for a 'Badge for Bravery'!

The carpet of moss and heather now became marshy ground into which my feet sank, swallowing my shoes forever. Reaching the top of the valley and the road, I had to endure almost all of the next twenty-six miles of the most circuitous route possible to Enniskerry, barefooted. Having started at the lakes of Poulaphuca, we continued up the mountains until we reached the Feather Beds. On through Glencree Valley we walked until we eventually reached Enniskerry. A few miles before reaching this destination, we visited Louis MacNeice's wife who lived in a little cottage. Delighted to accept her kind offer of tea, I was even more delighted to accept her even kinder offer of a pair of tennis shoes. Though two sizes too large for me, they greatly helped me on the rest of our journey of three miles to the Dublin bus. I think the entire walk took us twelve hours in total! Noel, amused by my predicament, remembered this particular outing for many years, silently admiring my stoicism.

I gradually learnt to be ready for anything in the future, as Noel never seemed to notice or care whether it was day or night, raining or sunny, time to eat or sleep! I looked upon his behaviour as that of a young, untrained pony which, when it felt like it, would kick up its heels, race off in any direction, full of gaiety, no thought for the morrow.

Dark Clouds

One afternoon in September 1938, Noel called to my home, suggesting we go out for a talk. Off we went in his tiny Austin to the 'Greyhound' where we had often spent many happy hours. Noel's mood, I could tell, was serious, and quickly I realised there was a good reason for this. I had been having trouble with my back, not enough to worry me, yet I had been advised to have it x-rayed. This, Noel quietly told me, holding my hand, had shown that one of my spinal bones was infected with tuberculosis. I would have to lie up immediately.

With sad quietness I took the news. What would happen to our friendship now? Would this finish it forever? Indeed, might I die? Tuberculosis had troubled my mind for many years, as it did most people's. Everyone had a friend or relation with the dreaded disease, and a month seldom passed by without hearing of the loss of a friend from the illness, a young school friend, the local shoemaker, the breadman who sat in all weathers on top of his horse-drawn van, and the milkman, equally open to the elements. From an early age I was aware of and constantly watching for the signs — loss of weight, pale, tired faces, endless coughing. It was impossible to ignore thoughts of contracting it. Bone tuberculosis, however, was different in that one's appearance changed very little, if at all, the infection being in the bone. One had to just rest whatever bone was damaged, sometimes for years.

Returning home from our sad meeting in the Greyhound to an empty house, for my parents were on their annual holiday in England, I took a long look at myself in the mirror. Nothing seemed changed, yet I shed a few self-pitying tears.

Within a few days I was in my hospital bed, in a ward of no less than twenty-two other patients, where I found a disagreeable lack of my precious privacy. After a few days of measuring my body from top to toe, I was horrified at the sight of an extraordinary contraption being carried towards my bed. This was my 'cage'. Depending on one's bone trouble, every patient was trapped in a cage of a different shape, the main justification for this discomfort being to prevent any movement of the body whatever, except for the arms and head. Like an innocent victim being thrown into a prison cell, I could only surrender in disbelief. With the large window by my bed always open, no matter what the weather, I lay there for a year.

Many patients were far more ill than I. A few young girls died of meningitis, while the girl beside me had been on her frame for seven years, with spinal trouble. This news made my heart sink. The long nights passed with the most distressing sounds, filled with the weeping, even screeching, of young mothers, missing their children at home.

Amid all the agony, unable to sleep, I lay watching the moon as it passed my window, remembering with sadness the happier times, when Noel and I had watched it together while it travelled over the hills of Wicklow, as he sang a few lines about "giving me the moon to play with".

The nurses were kind, but the rules they had to keep were, to my mind, punishing — enamel basins of cold water for washing oneself arrived at five-thirty in the morning; breakfast, tea from an enormous teapot, appeared around eight o'clock, accompanied by a couple of thinly buttered pieces of sliced bread. Patients like myself whose family lived in the city were luckier than the majority, who were from the country, for I could enjoy an egg now and then, brought to me by visitors.

As long as Noel visited me, as he did every day, I could bear the straitjacket existence, and hoped for the best. In a letter which he also wrote every morning, he reassured me he was never going to leave me, no matter what the outcome. What a pity that the large box of our letters to one another, often interesting, was lost on one of our many house moves in later years.

At last, after a year or so, the great day came when I was given the news that my x-ray was clear, and I could get out of my frame. Naturally I was very stiff and weak, for we had changed position just once weekly by being set on a plaster cast the exact shape of the frame and turned over, a manoeuvre which had enabled me to wash my hair! Happily surprised beyond belief for myself, though sorry for all those left behind, I found in a few weeks I could walk again. Pain once gone, is easily forgotten, and, in the innocence of youth, we believed that the future could never again be so bad. Summer came around, and we were once more enjoying life, though in a quieter way.

My stay in hospital, and Noel's experience as a student and later as a doctor, helped us realise more than ever the awful tragedies tuberculosis caused. We talked of the future, when Noel would have more experience, how we would together try to improve the awful conditions which so many suffered, conditions which he and his family had lived and died through in his very young days.

We still enjoyed our simple pleasures, especially sitting in that remarkable oasis, Trinity's cricket field, and later strolling to the Bailey where we could sit upstairs in the peace of the little 'back room'. Enjoying Guinness and sandwiches, we solved all the problems of the world – all, that is, except those that were to meet us in the future.

A Doctor at Last

Noel never worked really hard at his medical studies, preferring to enjoy himself. He was sure that with only three weeks of serious study, together with the photographic memory he believed he had, he could earn sufficient marks to pass his examinations; as he always did — even if he only passed with fifty-one marks, that was enough. Most of the other students in his years would study much harder, but, as I observed later, they did not necessarily become any better doctors than Noel.

At last Conferring Day 1941 arrived, when he could wear his gown, have his name loudly called out by the College Provost with the other successful new doctors, standing in the Square. What a happy proud feeling I had watching from the steps of the Chapel. Parties aplenty were arranged for that evening in celebration, but, as usual, we chose to spend it together in our own quiet enjoyable way: a drive through our hills and a meal in one of our Wicklow haunts.

Noel had been an intern student in Dr Steevens' Hospital, at Heuston Station, as part of his training. Now he was ready to return there as house physician to learn more practical medical duties such as theatre work, surgery et cetera. This interest and responsibility he enjoyed; it was a pleasant old building and he happily settled in, having his own room and his meals being provided.

All the same, there were more dark clouds on the horizon which neither of us expected. Life was becoming ever more serious.

Even Darker Clouds

My parents were so relieved that I had recovered from my experience in hospital that, for the first time, I was being treated with great care: breakfast in bed, rest in the afternoon, a short walk with Chico, my pet dachshund in the afternoons, and meeting Noel whenever he was free, in the evenings, when we might go to one of our haunts for a meal, or a walk in the Phoenix Park near Noel's hospital.

But a noticeable change in Noel's appearance began to worry me. He was losing weight, but I persuaded myself that this was because he was burning the candle at both ends, working and playing too hard. When first we met, Noel was tall, broad-shouldered, of fine physique, fond of playing squash, horse-riding, sailing and rugby. Still I wondered were we being visited again by the ever haunting fear of more illness? We were.

One gloomy afternoon my foreboding ended when a mutual friend called to tell me Noel was lying in the Richmond Hospital, and wished to see me. "Get me out of this awful place," he pleaded, "but stay with me." Aware of the seriousness of his situation, he was fearful, as he knew what was facing him, lying in a dilapidated dreary city hospital, in which nobody ill should have had to lie. I felt so sad for him, so used to comfort. We found a comfortable bed for him temporarily in the home of the family he had lived with on his return to Ireland, but knowing exactly what his symptoms meant, my words of comfort could not help him. The secret, insidious nature of tuberculosis had caught up with him, and no cure or relief whatever was known at this time.

Within a few days, Noel's appearance had already changed, his pale drawn face had no sign of a smile, just the look of a drowning man pleading "Save me". Visiting him, 'hidden' in his top-storey bedroom, I had a definite feeling of disapproval from the lady of the house — no welcoming smile at the opening of the door. Most distressful of all for Noel was the refusal of the servant to carry his meal tray upstairs to him. The fear of catching the disease was so real.

I went home, hid in my bedroom, and sobbed for hours, thinking that Noel's situation could only get worse. But on my next visit to him he had become a little more cheerful. He felt that he would be much less worried if he were in his 'own' hospital. This admission was quickly arranged and within a few days he was a patient in Dr Steevens' Hospital. There he had many friends to help him, who understood his illness. In Steevens', he settled, accepting his fate with more hope, but we both knew there was a long hard road in front of us.

A Long Journey to Happier Days

This hospitalization was the beginning of his many dreadful journeys from one hospital to another, one treatment to another — most of them painful and some even dangerous, lasting altogether six or so years. With his prodigious patience and courage, Noel fought the illness, recovering from time to time, but only for short periods. Each time we thought he might return to his old self, but again and again we were disappointed.

For the following six years, he lay in bed in the very hospital, strangely, in which I had lain on my steel frame a couple of years earlier. It was a case of visiting him, then a few month's respite, but then back to bed again, really ill. Crossing the old bridge over the Liffey at Kingsbridge which led to the Dr Steevens' Hospital, my heart would beat with anxiety, "Will I find him better today, or worse?" For months I crossed my 'Bridge of Sighs', trying to control my feelings, hoping against hope for a miracle.

Sick as Noel was, I could never bring myself to believe that the disease would win. He had extraordinary courage, this I always knew. Now that he was being looked after — as comfortable as it was possible for him to be — and as long as our relationship, and the security it seemed to give him, continued, there was always hope.

He spent most of his days reading books which I got for him from Switzer's Library. Just once we lost heart, when he went to England for treatment unavailable here; a most dreadful operation, which he knew very few patients survived. Asked would he care to see the priest before his operation, he refused.

So many of his friends at this time, probably thinking Noel was unlikely to survive, never tired of telling me I was 'silly' to wait for him, that I should forget him and enjoy life with them, dancing and partying. It was a dismal, sad part of my life, for hard as I tried, I could not enjoy life as I used to. Though I did have a certain amount of social life with his college friends, Noel's suffering would never let me free. He wrote constantly from England his thoughts on life and death, but I could do nothing to help ease him.

The Second World War was at a very serious stage by now, and it was difficult to get permission to travel to England, unless for employment. All we could do was wait until Noel's strength returned sufficiently to allow him to travel home to Dublin. After a long hard struggle, this he did, and we were together again. Though still weak, he resumed working for a higher medical degree, his M.D., which he passed, and with great relief and celebration we felt we could start again, looking to the future with optimism.

Remembering our plans made many years before, Noel now hoped, if his health allowed, to work in a few of the best British sanatoria, where he had had the benefit of treatment on and off during the years of his illness. Now he could continue to benefit from this care whilst also learning everything there was to know about tuberculosis, with the hope and intention of returning to Ireland with his experience. With a lighter heart than he had had for many years, he returned to England to an excellent sanatorium in Cheshire, and began to learn all he could with the finest doctors there.

Life's Journey Begun

Emigration, Wedding Bells and
Domestic Encounters

Even though England, especially London by 1943, was fighting for its life, after a few telephone calls from the GPO in Dublin (the only way then to communicate) we decided to waste no more time being separated. Although we never directly discussed the proposal of marriage, we always presumed that this would be our destiny. At that time in Ireland, it was considered very foolish to marry a person you knew to be suffering from tuberculosis. Also, having witnessed what had happened to his mother after his own father died from the disease, Noel feared for my future if the worst happened to him. Because of his fears, we had actually tried to part on a couple of occasions, but we always got back together after a short period, as being apart was a worse fate than an insecure future. Although others did not feel the same, and advised us so, we had faith that things would work out for us, difficult as we knew it might be. So when Noel asked me to join him in England, we silently acknowledged what the outcome of this journey would be — our wedding. After many weeks of form-filling, I finally got a passport and prepared to leave.

By now Noel was working in Harefield Hospital, Middlesex, a fine large new hospital where he could learn much useful knowledge, not only in tuberculosis, but also in surgery and general medicine, as the war-injured forces who could no longer be accommodated in St

Mary's Hospital in the city, were removed to Harefield for treatment.

Now that I had my precious passport, I felt secure enough about the immediate future to start sewing a few garments for myself, as well as sell my cheap watch and my violin. With the windfall all this produced, I bought a twenty-one carat wedding ring in a pawnshop in Capel Street for £3. What else could I wish for? I had no regrets, and even though my family were displeased at my leaving home a week before my sister had arranged to be married, nothing could change my mind or arrangements.

With the shortage of petrol at this time, one could not rely on a taxi. So, afraid that I might miss the boat train at Westland Row in the morning, I took no chance, and stayed overnight in a very downgrade hotel near the station. Dozens of young country boys, ill clad and hungry looking, clutching their few belongings in cardboard boxes and cases held together with string, anxiously milled around the hotel — each one, no doubt, full of hope of a good job in England. True to its name 'The Grand Hotel', we were served breakfast: bread, butter and a mug of tea, off a long wooden table, everyone side by side as in school, sitting on long wooden forms.

Gathering my own pathetic belongings in the morning, I joined the crowd crossing over to the station, anxious to get a seat on the train, which was clearly going to be packed. With no idea of exactly to where I was heading beyond London, I said a last goodbye to my only loyal girl friend, Daphne, wishing I could shout out for all to hear "I'm off to see Noel again!" Daphne, with whom I had spent many weekends at her home in Bray, was a good friend, but sadly we have since lost touch. Though I half-expected to see at least one of my parents on the platform to bid me goodbye — after all I was going to a 'war zone' — neither turned up. Still I had no pity for myself, though I should have been at least apprehensive, for I had never before travelled alone, and had little money in my pocket.

The train and boat were indeed packed to their limits, everyone half-excited, half-nervous with the wonder and worry of what the future held for them — I could see it on their faces, and hear their chat while they smoked incessantly.

I was glad to meet a few Trinity boys on the Holyhead train, on their way to join the forces as doctors; the journey passed quickly and pleasantly, and I felt safe in their company. Arriving at Euston, however, I felt tired and hungry, ill at ease with the new sounds and the eerie 'blackout' of the surroundings. To my surprise and delight, my brother's wife, Daphne Harrison, was at the exit, just as I was beginning to worry as to where to go next. Married to my brother Brian, who was by this time a prisoner of the Japanese in Changai Jail, she herself had escaped and now worked in London. An exceptionally beautiful lady, and clever, she held an important position and so was one of the few who were allowed a car, into which she now bundled me, explaining that having had a telegram from Dublin about my plans, she had come along with her mother to collect me.

For the moment life seemed to be going smoothly, and my first evening was spent in the comfort of my sister-in-law Daphne's flat in the centre of London, with the luxury of a hot bath — two inches of water allowed — a soft warm bed and a deep untroubled sleep. Before leaving for her work in the morning I was treated to breakfast in bed. "This is the last you'll have in bed for a long time," she said, and she was right.

Our Wedding Day

Next morning, Noel's sisters called to bring me to the underground station and out to the suburban London town where the Catholic Church was, the wedding arrangements having already been made for that day. In a really thick fog, even for London, we started on our journey, the most important of my life, so long awaited. It had taken almost eight worrying — though often strangely happy — years to get to this point in my life.

The fog and several air-raids held us up, but also gave us time for conversation, as this was the first time we had met. A remark made by a relation back in Ireland came back into my mind: "Pity she has to marry a Trinity Pape." I thought I had left all this sort of narrow-mindedness behind me until one of my future sisters-in-law gave me the feeling that she was not entirely happy with her brother's choice. "You've still time to change your mind," she advised me. "Do you understand what you're taking on?" and so forth. Clearly, at least with these girls, I was going to be a disappointment, for I quickly discerned that they would have preferred Noel's choice to be of his own faith.

How little they understood him, I thought, for the religious beliefs of others never bothered or interested him, nor had the subject ever become a topic of conversation between us. I wondered what the future held for me with these girls.

Due to air-raids, which forced the train to stop, and the thick fog, we arrived three hours late at the Church. A small group of guests, none of whom I knew, greeted us at the church door, but I had eyes for Noel only, as he smiled at me. Looking at him I had a mixture of feelings, not quite what I expected. After all the years of waiting for this day, here I was at last, so how could I feel anything but relief and happiness? Yet, one quick look at Noel and I saw an obviously ill man. I knew in my sinking heart that our life together from now on, as in past years, was not going to be easy.

The dangers of our staying together, of waiting for this day, had been obvious and had been explained to us by many well-meaning friends, nurses and doctors, even by Noel himself. Yet neither of us could part for life. Thus I could now only vow to myself that, with all my might and determination, I would care for him and make him strong again. Surely it would be possible if I looked back and remembered what a fine strong young man he had been, and of his courage when confined to bed, really ill, for so many months. I had faith in my eventual success; meanwhile, rest, good food and security would be essential.

With greetings over, we went into the Church which was quite empty; no flowers, no music, no prettily dressed bridesmaids, no confetti. Indeed, no sign of a priest, while we sat in silence for an hour. I wondered what was happening, as my mind wandered to home, not with any desire to be there, but with a vague wish that I could be in a more secure situation. My sister would be preparing for her wedding in a few days, to take place in the Church I had attended with my family for many years; where everything would be familiar to her, with countless members of the extended family and friends to wish her well. She would be wearing a long white dress, ribbons and bows, a large bouquet of flowers. Bridesmaids would be attending to her, each dressed in a pretty coloured dress, the organist playing the wedding march, photographers snapping, and the final happy reception, wedding cake and honeymoon.

But not for long did my dreaming last. I was beside the only person in the world I wished to be beside. We both knew that nothing could ever separate us except the 'grim reaper'. What matter if I was not wearing a conventional wedding dress, but only a simple suit?

As a little girl of five years, I had been one of six bridesmaids to my brother when he married with all the trimmings, in St Patrick's Cathedral. All my brothers had lavish weddings of this sort, but did it make any difference in their lasting? I think not, as after some years each one of them broke up with their wives, then re-married, leaving the sad remnants of hurt children behind. I know, though, that the effects of their war experiences were in part to blame.

Still waiting in the church, I became more anxious, until the priest arrived at last, full of apologies. He had been unable to trace the Registrar, due to the fog and bomb damage. Without him no certificate of marriage could be issued. The ceremony had to be postponed to the next day, not a good beginning I thought. Still, as though the marriage had taken place, our little group in the church then gathered in the flat where Noel and I were going to live (at £3 weekly rent). Kind nurses of Harefield Hospital had arranged a small party of welcome there, and we did not wish to let them down. A wartime wedding cake took pride of place on the table centre, (its recipe a few spoonfuls of dried egg, moistened with dried milk, baked and then decorated with pink icing), while buns and sardine sandwiches with a cup of tea completed the 'feast'.

The ceremony went smoothly next day, however. Because of the change of date, neither the doctor who was to give me away, nor the best man could attend; the doctor, having found the bottle of Irish whiskey which I had brought over for celebrations, 'went missing' for a week, and the best man had had to return to his war duties. So the landlady's sons kindly took their place.

The knot was tied! The only bells that chimed on this special day took the form of a small present given to me by an aunt: a bell for summonsing servants! Well-intended, I'm sure, but never used!

Settling Down, Browne Style!

With the service over at last, we started our life together in a small flat a few miles away from the hospital. Living conditions were difficult for everyone, with the shortage of housing and food. Our landlady, a widow, rented every room in her home, a pleasant old-fashioned bungalow, with a large garden in which she grew many types of vegetable and kept rabbits and hens for table.

Near an American Air Force base, it took me some time to get used to the night noises of aeroplanes, bombers and sirens, especially when Noel was on hospital duty and I was alone. At these dangerous times the good landlady, who slept in the ground floor, would bang on her ceiling with her walking stick, a sign for me to go downstairs to keep her company.

I would find her sitting upright in her untidy bed, wrapped in a once white shawl over her shoulders. Her hair, grey as her shawl, was covered with a frilly lace cap. How she spent her forced waking hours was extraordinary — sticking mirrors into powder boxes. To make the mirrors stick quickly onto the compacts, she'd give a little jump and sit upon them, hurrying up the process.

To help myself keep my mind off the commotion outside, I was willing enough to help her until I could go back to my bed in safety. Two of her precious fresh eggs, or perhaps a bunch of her precious asparagus, would be left on the window-sill at the end of the stairs next morning as a welcome 'Thank You'. During times like this, my feelings for those in the actual fighting above us were so mixed, no matter for which country those young men were risking their lives; German or English, American or French, each one was, in general, simply a victim obeying his superiors. I felt so sorry for them, and their loved ones, awaiting for news of them. I was glad not to have been born a man! When will we ever learn that problems are never solved by war?

Meanwhile, Noel kept working busily in the hospital, trying with his colleagues to keep up with the rush of injured, some indescribably wounded, who arrived day after day. The English people, we thought, were remarkable; so uncomplaining, always courteous, going about their business no matter now awful the news.

Hungry for music, we occasionally took a chance and went to a recital or symphony concert in the city. Indeed, despite the various uncertainties of travelling, when Noel had a free day we would take a bus to any town with the remotest rural ambience, and enjoy a walk. Our flat was so small, and without any sort of comfort, that we felt like two wild animals needing freedom, and simply had to escape, even for a few hours.

When we felt like dancing, the best we could do was to go out to the flat concrete roof of the kitchen, put a record on the old wind-up gramophone, shut our eyes and pretend we were in the Metropole or Gresham in Dublin. Enfolded, we would drift-dance as we had long ago, wishing our youth, and especially Noel's health, would last. Age is a bothersome thing, a withering curse like ill-health, which never seemed to leave our minds for long.

But we were so ecstatically happy to be together, every day was a bonus. For the first time in his life, since he was twelve years of age, Noel was only now realising what security, both physical and emotional meant; what it was like to live naturally without being under an obligation or compliment to anyone for anything. As the old song went: 'He ate when he was hungry, and drank when he was dry'. I believe that just because you are married, you do not own your partner. We did not believe that either of us had to change our ways to please one another; we were both free souls, yet fortunately wholly dependent on one another. What one lacked, the other supplied. We thrived like plants in each other's garden.

An Irresistible Offer

We were settling happily into our new way of life when Noel was invited quite unexpectedly to return to the hospital in Co Wicklow where he had worked before for some years, only this time as Acting Superintendent. Now we were faced with yet another major change, which had to be seriously considered. Noel's health had greatly improved, and he was happier than he had been for years, in both his medical work and home life. I wondered would the change to Ireland be wise?

But there was really no problem in making up our minds, as we had always planned to return. By this time the war was almost over, if one could be sure a war is ever truly over and won, so we had no feelings of guilt. Romantic as ever, we felt the hills of Wicklow, the River Liffey, and the Abbey Theatre all called us back. We could have it both ways we thought, in work and pleasure.

With our belongings packed into two small cases, for we had collected little else but experience in our time in Harefield, we bade goodbye to the many pleasant working friends we had made, and started our journey home. Staying in a London city hotel near Euston Station, we had a sleepless night, the window panes having crashed into the bedroom just before we arrived. Glad to board the morning train from Euston to Holyhead, we enjoyed a few catnaps. While Noel slept on the boat for a while, I climbed to the top deck, waiting for my first view of the hills of Dublin and Wicklow. What joy! I called Noel to join me. "You're not sorry?" he asked, knowing we were leaving security and interesting work behind. Neither of us were at that moment, but what lay ahead?

Arriving at the dusty, gloomy station of Westland Row, we took a hansom cab to my home, an experience we had promised ourselves and looked forward to even before leaving London. As a student in Dr Steevens' Hospital, Noel would sometimes treat himself to a horse and cab drive along by the Liffey to the hospital, immensely enjoying the sound of the horses' hooves, making their clippity-clop sounds on the cobbles.

Now back in Dublin and together, we trotted off to my home. Glad to see us safely home, my mother had a pleasant meal ready for us after which we left for Wicklow, longing to settle into our new home, with Chico, our delighted dachshund, who had been looked after by my mother while we were away.

Back in Newcastle

Arriving at the hospital, and being greeted by our old friends, we felt that, without doubt, this would be a far more pleasant way of life — at least domestically. Our new home was to be a pretty gate lodge on the hospital grounds, set in a large garden, with the hills of Wicklow in the background. Tall trees housed crows and pigeons, whose busy sounds woke us at morning. Since Noel had already worked here as a junior doctor a few years before we married, I would have visited him in those faraway days by taking a train to Greystones, walking some miles from there by the railway tracks beside the sea to

Newcastle Station, and then along the country lanes leading to the hospital, a walk of almost ten miles. Now, after our adventures, here we were again, but together in our own home, just five minutes walk away from Noel's patients, making it possible for him to get home during the day for his essential rest.

We were very happy at how things were working out and imagined ourselves enjoying many years living there. But it was not to be. Quickly Noel noticed that nothing in the medical department had improved during the years he had been away. Books, reports, even medicine bottles were still in the same position, obviously unused. It took us some time to realise that everything in the garden was not as rosy as it seemed, and in time, working hard with little success, he naturally became frustrated. It was a small hospital, with all the beds occupied, but with a waiting list of about 1,000 patients a year. It was heartbreaking to realise that the recovery rate of the patients was far less than the death rate.

With the experience he had gathered in Welsh and English sanatoria, it was evident to Noel that he must quickly try to make improvements. Tuberculosis in Ireland at that time was accepted as the 'will of God', making it difficult to find anyone who would show some sort, any sort, of interest or willingness to get involved and make things better.

After months of meetings with various groups — trade unions, medical and even religious groups — no useful interest was shown. An organised national programme, run by the State, on the same successful lines as the British welfare state at that time, was the only way

Noel could see which would help make the necessary improvements.

But this would mean political action and how could Noel get into politics? As in a jigsaw, the necessary piece turned up by chance.

Into the Jaws of Politics

The Political Spark Ignites — 1947

A lawyer, Noel Hartnett, was one day visiting the hospital where a friend of his was lying extremely ill. The patient was a gentle man, a journalist in *The Irish Times*, who needed special attention only the visiting doctor from Dublin could provide. But, because the patient could no longer afford the attention he needed, he was just left to bear his illness unattended. Extremely cross at seeing his patient being treated like this, Noel, along with Noel Hartnett, arranged that the good colleagues of the journalist collected enough money in the *Times* office to send him to London for the necessary operation.

Unfortunately the poor man died under his operation. This dreadful experience distressed both Noels so much that they had long talks together, determined that this cruel behaviour would not happen again. Had that patient had money for the doctor, he might not have died.

Already steeped in politics, Noel Hartnett decided that my Noel should try for a Dáil seat in the next General Election, as a member of the new political party, Clann na Poblachta, being started by Sean MacBride. The promise of improvements in the tuberculosis services would be part of Noel's sincere request for votes. Most people, at that time, had a family member or friend ill, and unlikely to recover from the disease. Mr Hartnett thought that people would be glad to vote for someone

89

whom they believed to be serious and sincere in his intentions.

Here was the opportunity for which Noel had been wishing since he started his medical career, an absolutely unthought of and unexpected answer to his ambition regarding the elimination of tuberculosis, a struggle which had been going on for thousands of years.

Always with the thought at the back of our minds that the people might not vote for a completely unknown candidate, Noel and I talked over the idea together, time and again. Working hard in the hospital was one thing, but working as a public representative, if he were to be successful, was quite another. It would be a case of making a real sacrifice, for there was always the thin line to be considered between Noel's health and ill-health. How would he stand up to such a change, such strain?

After our talks (and worries) of the chances he would be taking, and the hoped-for result if he were successful, we decided that, in duty, we should try. After all, this was the reason for the lives we had been living in the previous years, indeed since Noel had qualified: to improve the standard of care for the patients, *all* patients, with tuberculosis.

I knew that Noel was a conscientious organiser as well as an excellent doctor, and that there were 'so many ill, so few caring'. If he could keep well, I felt, it was a wonderful opportunity, although at the back of my mind I could not forget the doctor's quiet words at our wedding, when he said to me, in a pitying tone of voice, "You'll be lucky if you still have him for much more than six months" — though, in truth, I had been aware of this possibility myself.

But that had been a few years before. If we decided to go along with this new proposition, our idea was that I would look after the domestic side of our lives, look after our financial problems as best I could, and always be on hand no matter what hour of the day or night, to have a meal ready for him — for he disliked eating out — and spend whatever spare time we could find talking over and solving the day's problems, if any.

I feel that today's feminists might be appalled at this arrangement, but it was our way of doing the best we could to allow Noel to do his work with as little stress as possible, as rest was essential to prevent his tuberculosis recurring.

We waited, having made all plans we possibly could, to be ready for the next General Election, expected sometime in 1948. Noel had a lot to learn, and Noel Hartnett was willing to help him all he could. We both had a pathetic idea of how democracy worked — or was meant to work. I even had to think twice before making my mind up as to whether a political idea was of the 'left', or of the 'right'. I was sure only of what was wrong and what was correct in how people were being treated, and I had a great desire to rectify matters. This new life, I felt, was going to be well worth living if Noel had any luck at all and kept well.

The Pitter-Patter of Tiny Feet

Meanwhile our quiet domestic life continued happily, with the addition now of two daughters, angelic human beings. Before our marriage we had decided that we certainly would not be wise to have a large family, such as Noel's had been. We were taking a serious enough decision in being married anyway, and it was a constant worry of Noel's as to how I would manage if he were to die young of his tuberculosis, as was quite possible, even probable.

Our first daughter, Ruth, had been born on an icy cold day in January 1945, within a couple of years of our having married. I had to go to Dublin where a bed had been booked for me in a small nursing home. The head doctor's wife happened to be travelling to Dublin a day or two before our daughter was due to be born, and offered to take me with her.

She dropped me near a bus terminus in Dublin, which would bring me fairly near to my home, where I would stay with my parents. I was anxious, indeed frightened, at having to cross the road to the bus stop, for the ground was thick with ice, dangerous to walk on. By myself, carrying a case of necessities, I wondered at how a lady who has given birth to six or seven children could not understand my fearful feelings, and help me to at least get across the icy road? However, the bus brought me across the city, where I again had to carefully walk the ten-minute distance on ice to reach my home.

Relieved at last to be safe, after taking some refreshment, I went to bed. Without a phone at that time Noel knew not what was happening. But later, when all was revealed, he very upset to hear of the needless worry and difficulties I had had, having presumed I would have been driven to my door by the doctor's wife.

Next morning I knew that I should go to the nursing home, but this arrangement did not work out easily either. Finally my father went off to find a taxi. With nervous farewells my parents and I waved goodbye, while I wondered why my mother did not come to help me? In absolute innocence of what was before me, I arrived at the nursing home, to be told they had no bed for me.

How was it, I wondered, that whatever arrangement we made rarely worked out easily? All our friends had their children born without any hitch: they arrived on time in whatever nursing home they had chosen, spent a comfortable two-weeks rest in large well-furnished rooms, with pretty frilled curtains, and vases of flowers sent by well-wishers on every side, the new-born always cosily wrapped up in a cradle.

A bed was eventually found for me in an old house in Mount Street run by two kind sisters, who would not charge us any fee. Did we look that 'down and out', I still wonder? Noel came as soon as he could, so pleased that all was over. Since working as a student of midwifery in the Rotunda Hospital, he disliked attending births. Remembering one of his cases which he had had to attend to at that time still horrified him. He found the lady, who lived in one of our slum areas in Dublin, in a single room on the top floor, with a cock and a few hens for company! He did his best, but the picture stayed with him during the debate on the service he wanted when in politics later on — a service for mothers and their children. Thinking back on this poor lady in a cock loft, I felt, despite my few problems, grateful and happy with my lot, my comparative comfort.

I had my own ideas on how to bring up our daughters, believing from the very beginning that a trusting relationship must be built up between parents and child; no 'carers', no *au pairs*, no play-schools at three years of age. Ruth was a contented happy child anyway, giving us both great interest and joy, as we watched her every new step in growing up. Noel spent every available moment he could find with her. They would meet, as soon as she learnt to walk, halfway between the hospital and the house when it was time for Noel to come home, and together they would take a little walk around the local fields, chatting all the way as they watched for the different flowers and birds. Neither Noel nor I believed in corporal punishment, but rather in the Chinese saying: "Never allow your children to feel they have lost their dignity." Play was education of a kind: how to hold a scissors when cutting out pictures, to open drawers while looking for something without pinching fingers, how to fit the correct size lids on pots, et cetera. All simple and cheap!

Our second daughter Sue was born a couple of years later, in 1947 — quite a different personality, but as angelic as her sister. She was born in the Rotunda Hospital where neither of us had much comfort, for as with Ruth, there was no bed for me, and I spent one day and night lying on a trolley in a corridor, cold and anxious, listening to the screams of poor Dublin women, likely already mothers of five or six small children, swearing at their husbands in language I had never heard before.

I was eventually offered a 'private' bed, after Sue's birth, but I refused, as I wished to see how one was treated in a public ward — I was not impressed. I didn't like Sue being left to cry without attention, and worse still I got ill with an abscess and had to send the poor child home and remain for two-weeks treatment in the hospital. During those two weeks Sue was kindly looked after at home by one of the hospital nurses, but when I saw her on my return, I went out to the garden, weeping to Noel, "Sue is not going to live, she's grey, thin, and will not stop crying."

The fact was that Sue was simply hungry, or so I hoped, as I sent someone racing to the village to buy a tin of 'Cow and Gate' food. This worked wonderfully. She drank bottle after bottle, nine one night, and quickly became stronger. She is still making up for those two weeks hunger yet!

On the subject of crying children, I have never been able to bear hearing a child in distress. Once in a railway station in Howth, many years ago, Noel helped a young girl to lift her crying baby and pram into the train. I stayed aboard with her a moment longer, trying to console the child, who was really upset. She was crying so hard that I did not hear the train whistle blow, and so found myself moving off in the train, leaving Noel, Ruth and Sue on the platform, making signs that they'd catch up with me at the next station and collect me! Still it was a successful journey, for the child had stopped crying by the time we met up again. There was a lesson for me here somewhere, perhaps not to interfere with other people's domestic problems. I know I'll never change this habit, though — one can't teach a old dog new tricks.

I cannot imagine life without our daughters and their children, and the many joys they have always given us. Nobody could be moved more by the sight of a newly born infant than I, yet a feeling of sadness comes over me when I see their little innocent faces. I think of the traumas they will inevitably face in their future, though I am thankful they are healthy. All one can do is prepare them as best as possible. I found that forming a child's mind can be a most interesting and important role for a parent, so that they will grow up to be well-integrated citizens, with the social attitudes which will help them to lead a useful life for themselves and society in general. At least, if they meet up with difficult personal problems in their own lives, as did both our daughters, they might survive these with understanding and less stress. But unless a good relationship has been built up between parent and child, this is unlikely to happen. To remain a constant but unobtrusive companion may mean less unnecessary suffering for the child and for the adult in later life. Yet we've known many girls who, when they've been unlucky in their marriage, are told by their parents, "You've made your bed, now lie on it", a cruel attitude.

Regretfully, I am not a trained child psychologist, but I would like to have studied the subject when young. I just go my way by instinct more than anything else, but by whatever way, our daughters are truly good people — unselfish, thoughtful, good company with a sense of humour; honest and honourable.

We were always aware and thankful that our young daughters were healthy and happy. Our only worry was finance, but with care we managed, though I would have liked to have had a pram which did not constantly lose one of its wheels when I was taking a walk on the country roads. I could always recover it, but it must have meant a sudden jolt for the poor child in the pram.

It was when my children grew up that they, and even myself, realised that not everyone is brought up with the same social attitudes and beliefs — differences

In my garden, Cabra Road, with Chico the Dacshund, 1938.

Phyllis (left), Evelyn and Roderic in the garden of 25 Cabra Road, c. 1929.

On holidays in the Isle of Man, 1937.

Holidaying in Donegal, with parents, 1939.

With Chico and Puss, in Bray, 1960.

The famous photo of Noel being attacked by an Alsation at a protest march to the US Embassy in Ballsbridge, which appeared on the cover of The Irish Times, 24 October, 1962.

Photo by Gordon Standing, courtesy of The Irish Times.

A young Sue.

Outside the house in Malahide, 1990.

Noel and myself dancing, Christmas 1993.

Cutting the cake at our surprise fiftieth
wedding anniversary party, 1994.

Ruth, 1998.

At my brother Roderic's seventieth birthday party, (from left) myself, Noel, Roderic
and his wife Dearbhal.

Noel is awarded a Fellowship by Trinity college, May 1994. (from left) Glyn, myself, Noel and Ruth.

Sailing 'the Wag' in Connemara.

Family and friends gather after Noel's funeral, May 1997, including grandchildren, Cormac (far left), Glyn (third from left), Ruairi (next), and Nena (second from right): and daughters Sue (beside Ruairi) and Ruth (sitting on ground).

which can eventually lead to difficulties. This is why I cannot agree that a mother should go out to work, leaving her children to someone else to be cared for while she's away. I know that some couples feel that for financial reasons they must do this, but I think it's fairer to the child to be looked after by the mother — and more natural.

The Reluctant Warrior Goes into Battle, 1948

Half-excited, half-scared, Noel found himself at last being thrown in at the deep end of politics. Early in 1948, a General Election was called, and he was selected to stand as a candidate in Clann na Poblachta. With the decision having been made many months before, we put all worries behind us, and started yet another completely new and different life. Having been out of Ireland for ten years, Noel had had to catch up with a lot of political information. For instance, he initially knew absolutely nothing about Sean MacBride's political background, but had become interested by the fact that MacBride was aware that tuberculosis was a worrying issue in the country, and was willing to take a candidate who was seriously interested in eradicating it, while at the same time helping to build up the new party.

With the help of many wonderful hard-working friends, many of them ex-patients, the campaign was successful, after three weeks of gruelling hard work. Were it not for the dozens of helpers, who worked from a flat in the city — kindly given over for the campaign by a good friend — and many energetic students who non-stop, day and night, climbed ladders to tie posters onto lamp-posts, Noel might not have been so lucky.

The fact was that one essential part of political life, public speaking was anathema to Noel, one experience which he did not at all enjoy. It took him some time even before he felt comfortable speaking in public; it was against his personality, but he knew he had to persist to make his points. Also, he greatly disliked the idea of disturbing families by knocking on their doors, and would never ask directly for a vote, but just explain what he wanted to do, and how. To have to stand at corners of his constituency on an old, flag-bedecked lorry, making the necessary speeches while those who opposed him heckled noisily from the footpath was, he felt, a primitive, undignified way to get his ideas across to his listeners. As for myself — listening to him on the few occasions I could get to Dublin from our home in Newcastle — I was equally unhappy, for a microphone was not available, and to hear him straining his precious lungs in order to be heard was worrying.

When the three weeks of campaigning were over, the dreaded day of the count came, a day Noel always avoided as best he could. His friends would watch the counting of his votes, while he wandered around the museums and galleries, and paid visits to his "down the line" antique dealers, where he would enjoy discovering small treasures to bring home — maybe a copper kettle, an old oil lamp or ornament. Our very good friend Jack McQuillan, a TD, sadly gone from us recently, was very clever with the figures, and could tell early on in the count how Noel was likely to fare. Jack would phone me at home to relay the news, and in turn Noel would phone me. Sometimes this nerve-wracking day would go on into the night. Remarkably on that, his first experience, the good people of Dublin South–East voted Noel into the

Dáil. Apprehensively we looked forward to our own new life, changed forever so quickly.

Down to Work — February 1948

Aware since first becoming ill that every day was precious, and no time was to be wasted, Noel got down to work straight away, knowing exactly what he needed to do — 'Flash' Browne as some of his colleagues named him! As Minister for Health on his first day in the Dáil, and being unusually young for such a position — thirty-two — I have little doubt that his fellow Cabinet Ministers considered him inexperienced (he was), too arrogant, omniscient and assertive (he was not), and always in a hurry and impatient of laziness. One newspaper even wondered was it advisable to take on a Minister who had been educated in England!

One could not blame other Ministers if they had a certain amount of distrust in him, as he was so new on the political scene, and they had had some years of experience. But the unusual life which Noel had lived up to this point surely gave him a certain courage and self-confidence. It was unlikely that any of them had skied on the snowy dangerous slopes of the Austrian mountains as Noel had as a student, or canoed many miles of European rivers, sleeping on their banks and living on black bread and cheese, for lack of money, or ridden in a point-to-point race. These adventures, enjoyed when he was young and healthy, together with the memories of his family's traumatic break-up through death from tuberculosis, strengthened his character and no doubt helped to give him the utterly passionate wish he had to succeed in this new opportunity to work for the tuberculosis patients.

After the Election

When the results were known, and the cheering had ended, photos taken and congratulations over, Noel realised that the price to be paid for success would be even higher than he thought. With so much to be done in political work alone, such as attending the Dáil every day, little time was left for family matters, and it worried him that the children might grow up with all the disadvantages of a one-parent family. These were the sacrifices we had not foreseen when having our conversations as to whether he should be a politician or not, and I am sure every politician's wife has the same problems as we had in our time.

However, we all 'battled on' at home, with my explanation of their father's absence to our daughters being that 'Noel was out building hospitals for sick people'. But his absence did affect them to an extent, for it all happened so suddenly — one day they were living their secure happy life with their two parents, the next day Noel was gone, away all day and most nights home late, shattering their little habits.

Meeting Mr MacBride

Still we thought at least that we could enjoy a holiday together, as usual in the West. With our two dogs and cats — they always had to be with us — we rented a cottage by the sea near Westport. Noel was glad to get a rest from the city, from the endless though satisfying work at the Department and the Dáil, and to have time for play with our daughters was sheer pleasure for him.

But we were not left in peace for long. Playing around in the garden we saw a large black car coming towards the cottage. We were not expecting visitors, for nobody, we thought, knew where we were staying. I will not easily forget my feeling of panic when I realised who was coming, for it was none other than Sean MacBride, with Mr Clement Attlee, the British Labour Party leader, and his colleague, Mr Noel Baker.

My immediate thought was 'What will I give them for lunch?' for it was early afternoon, and presumably they had not eaten. We raced into the cottage, throwing all the untidy bits and pieces into holes and corners, dusted our selves down, then greeted them with smiles. This was the first time I had met Mr MacBride. As he introduced his companions to Noel, I immediately felt that this man was unusual, not only in his appearance, but also in his behaviour and in his manners.

Of course Noel had often spoken of him and had been to his house in Roebuck, where I too would later meet his mother, Maud Gonne, then very old. On one occasion she showed me a book of photographs of Sean, of whom she seemed very proud. One small picture of him I remember clearly. He was only about ten years of age in it, maybe less, yet written over the picture were the words 'Sean, Man of Destiny'. The adoring mother had her son's future worked out for him! I wonder did he live up to her expectations?

MacBride looked interesting, that day in Westport, certainly not the least bit 'Irish', no healthy 'broth of a boy' complexion, but of sallow complexion and gaunt of face. He wore an air of seriousness, as though he was carrying the troubles of the world on his shoulders. I could see no sense of humour in his face, but he did display a little charm, at times — which I felt was false. This was maybe unfair, but I was quicker always than Noel to see through people.

In any case, my dilemma was still facing me: what to offer the visitors for lunch. A quick look through the kitchen gave me the disastrous answer; all I had was plenty of eggs, as we'd been lazy that morning and had not been to the nearest shop, which anyway sold only the basic necessities and was ten miles away. So it had to be omelettes, cooked on the open fire, which at least would be a novelty to them! While they sat around talking politics, after a few remarks on the pleasant smell the turf gave out, I got down to work, with Noel's help, and cooked what seemed dozens of eggs, spiced with herbs. To make a good impression I wore white gloves (*à la Française*) handling the hot plates, and, as the omelettes were cooked one by one, I urged the men to eat them immediately, so that they would not collapse. A bottle of wine, kindly brought to us by Mr Attlee, improved the atmosphere greatly.

Luckily, the very excellent hotel nearby produced a splendid dinner for us in the evening, making up for my miserable offering. During the hours our visitors were in our cottage I noticed, as their conversation continued, how Mr MacBride took absolutely no interest in our daughters, who were behaving very well. Nor indeed did he have anything to say to me: I might as well not have been there. I had never met such behaviour, and wondered what the reason for it was. It could have been just bad manners — that I did not matter — however it certainly was not because he disliked ladies, for Sean was well known as an admirer of ladies! Mr Attlee and Mr Noel Baker, however, were quiet well-mannered gentlemen, who appreciated my efforts.

Noel never became a close friend of Sean MacBride; wearing his psychiatrist's hat he put down the curious characteristics of the man to his unusual, and insecure childhood. To Noel, and most people, MacBride was a 'man of mystery', with his very broken French accent, his history of alleged violence when in the IRA, and his father who had been an executed martyr to the cause of Republicanism in Ireland.

I was with Noel when, continuing the visit with Mr Attlee, we called to Kylemore Abbey in Connemara. There I was as stunned almost as Noel to see how Mr MacBride, whom we never thought was religious, greet the Abbess on his knees, and kiss the ring on the lady's hand. Perhaps MacBride was really more a diplomat than a politician — maybe a mixture of both, for Noel noticed how careful he always was to impress people who were important, and to do the right thing, especially when it came to religious affairs.

With all the members of the Cabinet, MacBride went to Rome in the Holy Year 1950, and had his photograph taken at the opening of the Holy Door for the newspapers. Noel declined to go. I was beside Mr Lavery, the government's Attorney General, at a dinner when the subject of the 'Pilgrimage to Rome', as the affair was being called, was mentioned in our conversation. 'What day are you going to Rome?' he asked. I answered that I had no intention of going. I told him that I didn't consider getting into an aeroplane and travelling to Rome (top hat and tails in luggage) as a pilgrimage. I would consider taking part only if I walked, barefoot preferably, from here to there. 'You're not very practical,' was his answer, but I did think that the whole business was hypocritical.

When Mr MacBride had to travel abroad, which seemed to be quite often, Noel had to act as Minister for External Affairs, receiving notable visitors, and entertaining them to dinners. Neither of us enjoyed these affairs, unless, as was occasionally the case, somebody as interesting as Indian Prime Minister Pandit Nehru, Dr Fleming of penicillin fame, or Cardinal Cushing from the USA were the principal visitors. Cocktail parties were such a waste of time, in general, for as soon as one got into an interesting conversation, someone would come along and interrupt with stories of their latest holiday, their illnesses, new houses, and so on.

When in Dublin, however, Mr MacBride greatly enjoyed giving very grand dinners in the extravagantly furnished building of the Foreign Affairs Offices in St Stephen's Green. We had a secret sign when Noel wished to leave for home. Noel would take his specs off, shine them with his handkerchief while I'd watch, then off we'd go, disappearing without being noticed, down the back stairs!

The politicians, and especially their wives, gave me the impression that they greatly enjoyed these formal occasions, the ladies dressed in a different and expensive-looking gown each time. Our two daughters were still very young, needing continual attention, so my 'gown' had to be made by me in a hurry, between meals more or less, in one or two days. A pleasant neighbour used to be amused at seeing me in the coal shed in the afternoon, washing clothes or finishing my housework, and later, in the evening, leaving home in a long dinner dress, with the usual 'glamorous' extras — handbag and gloves.

Noel never used the ministerial car except when on his Departmental work. But it was sent to collect me on these special evenings, not having a car myself. The car was driven weekly in turn by two most pleasant gardaí, Harry and Joe, who became greatly loved and were always greeted with joy by Ruth and Sue. They were so obliging: one evening when driving me to town, Joe stopped to pick a rose hanging over a garden wall, with which to decorate my dress; another time, Harry stopped at a chemist shop to buy lipstick I had forgotten while I hastily took the tacking threads out of the hem of my newly made dress!

I have often wondered whether Noel should ever have joined Sean MacBride's party. If he had known the political background of Mr MacBride, I doubt if he would have had anything to do with him, for he abhorred violence. In his mixture of political innocence and naivety he joined the party with chiefly one purpose in mind, the hope of eliminating tuberculosis. And except for this success in reducing the disease, and exposing the hypocrisy of the Catholic Hierarchy, many of his years were largely wasted in trying to achieve, mainly on his own, further improvements and justice in social affairs.

But, of course, to be in government was a really wonderful opportunity for Noel, for which every tuberculosis patient was thankful, and I know in my heart that it was the right thing for him to have done. It's just that Noel, having learnt gradually the nature of his 'leader', was eventually shocked and disappointed.

Everyone in politics had heard talk of the violent life of MacBride, but Noel took no notice of these rumours until it was too late. In Noel's book, *Against the Tide*, he mentions how Sean MacEntee, a Minister in the Fianna Fáil government, disclosed how there were republican links with the Nazis, and how MacBride had been Chief of Staff of the Irish Republican Army up to the 1930s, connected with many attempted murders, and possible murders. When MacEntee charged MacBride with these facts, MacBride never made any attempt to defend himself against the charges by legal action. Noel was unknowingly in the lion's jaw, and was lucky to have escaped from being completely savaged.

How MacBride was given the Lenin Peace Prize, and the Nobel Peace Prize also, is a mystery to me, and many others.

Holidays

Our holidays in the West of Ireland, enjoyable because we were all together, became difficult for Noel as people stopped him in streets, shops, and the local hotel, to talk politics with him — just what he wanted to forget for a while.

For Noel to benefit from any change he would have to take a holiday out of Ireland, which was so small, and where everyone knew everyone. Two summers into his work at the Department, and after yet another bout of tuberculosis, he needed a rest badly. I talked my concerns over with Noel's secretary, who immediately made all arrangements for us to journey to Biarritz, in the South of France. We decided to travel by car, driving to Rosslare, then by boat to France, and overnight by car-train to Biarritz.

Packing our little Fiat car, the smallest on the market, with food we knew would be scarce on the Continent due to the war, which was only a few years over, we eventually started off on our journey. Noel's sister, who taught in New York at a school for children whose parents worked in the United Nations, would be pleased to take care of Ruth and Sue. They knew her well, for she visited us every summer for the three months or so in which her school was closed for holidays.

Off we went, not really excited, but knowing it was a sensible idea. I remember the very moment we looked at one another. It was outside the Church at Donnybrook, just as we were starting to drive on the Bray Road, for Rosslare. The same thoughts had entered each other's mind, at the same moment — we'd much prefer to tour Wicklow, and this is what we did. We spent a most wonderful day, stopping anywhere we liked for rest and refreshment. If we could have spent our holiday in this way, we would have been perfectly happy, as we had no desire to travel elsewhere. However, in time, we had to return home, to the amazement of the family, and feeling a little foolish.

Within a few days Noel's secretary, intent on Noel getting away, made arrangements for us once again to travel to Biarritz, but not by car. It was pleasant enough, though not really the kind of life we would choose for more than a few weeks — too crowded, too hot, too noisy, too expensive. But we did meet the Duke and

Duchess of Windsor, with a quick handshake and smile, which was something interesting to report when we returned home, even though it was a chance meeting — I think we were mistaken for some other, more important couple, in the night club we visited just once! In any case we returned home with delight, refreshed, and settled down again.

We very much preferred a visit we had years later in the mid-1980s to Moscow, where Noel was invited to speak to a university meeting, and attend an important Peace Conference arranged by Mr Gorbachev, who was also the chief speaker. I wondered how we would understand the language, but they had a clever idea whereby if you pressed the correct button on your chair arm — English, French, German, or whatever language you wished — his speech came through your earphones in your language of choice. The huge hall was full of artists, film stars, politicians, musicians, many of whom I could recognise from magazines, films, and television. I remember Gregory Peck sat in front of us, and nearby I spotted the great pianist John Ogolen.

Mr Gorbachev made a speech which I thought was wonderful, not unlike the 'Sermon on the Mount'. A charming man, I was really sorry when he was ousted a few years later. We were lucky to be invited to the Kremlin to join in a exchange of views with him and his ministers.

Moscow, even though so much of it was destroyed during the war, was still a beautiful city, as the old parts which had survived were proudly renovated. We could have lived there happily in its civilised ambience. No matter what time of day, one could always find a concert being performed, an art gallery, or many kinds of museums to visit, and of course the ballet.

We were full of admiration for the casual way the ordinary citizens appeared to accept the awful sufferings they had endured during their many years of war. I've always felt that but for their bravery and the dreadful losses they suffered, both men and women, we would not have won the war.

If we had had another life, this would be the place we'd have liked to live in, occasionally visiting the beautiful but sad city of Leningrad. As it was, one trip to Moscow ended our travels for evermore, except between Dublin and Galway.

Beginning of the Break-Up

It was inevitable that in time the coalition of 1948—1951 would disintegrate. There were so many disparate points of view, so little idealism. Given the mutual distrust between 'left' and 'right', and less interest in the public good than in their own positions, something had to give, for Clann na Poblachta and Fine Gael had nothing in common beyond a desire to get rid of Fianna Fáil for good. I believe the breakup started when Hartnett and MacBride travelled to America, Hartnett to write the scripts for MacBride. There emerged a conflict of interest, as MacBride's aim was to solicit American help over the partition problem by offering Northern Ireland as a base for their naval air-force, while Hartnett, though appealing to Irish-American republicans for help, was opposed to this mode of exchange.

After this journey in America, I understand that Hartnett's and MacBride's relationship collapsed, naturally leading eventually to the collapse of the Clann na Poblachta party. But there were a few battles to be fought before the whole coalition collapsed, the Mother and Child Scheme being the principal one as far as Noel was concerned. Unfortunately for Noel, Hartnett resigned from the party in February 1951, a serious blow to those who remained — for the few party members who realised his worth — though he continued to advise Noel.

Naturally I was only an onlooker at these times, and knew only how things were progressing through Noel, when he returned home at night and we sat up into the late hours, or the early hours of the morning, talking about the day's events and problems.

Strangely, no matter how black things were, we never took any notice of the infighting which went on between the various Ministers. Noel just kept working as hard as ever, pleased with the progress of his programme. The men who worked on the building of new hospitals, some of whom returned from their jobs in England to do so, worked through nights by the light of huge electric lamps. Beds for tuberculosis patients increased from less than 3,000 in 1932 to almost 6,500 in 1952. Together with the necessary support services — an x-ray service for everyone, to help sort out those who had the disease as early as possible, medical and nursing staff to look after the waiting patients, payment to help families whose wage-earner had to stay in bed, BCG inoculation and educational films — these helpful ideas at last brought down the rate of the once dreaded plague.

To my annoyance some people in the medical profession thought Noel was wasting money by building too many hospitals, as they would not be needed since new drugs were slowly coming onto the market. But, if it was a case of drugs only working the miracle, how is it that TB is still a huge problem in India and other third-world countries? Beds and services are required for complete treatment and rest in any country, as well as for other diseases, such as cancer; one often hears of people having to wait up to three or four years for a bed, so they can have a hip replacement, or some other surgery performed on them.

Still, I was so pleased, so glad that we had taken the risks we did, to see Noel's desire to get rid of tuberculosis become reality.

The Mother and Child Scheme 1950–1951

Noel's next serious campaign was to improve the lot of deprived and ill mothers and their children. As with tuberculosis he knew exactly what he needed to do from experience. He had seen the suffering in the city slums when a medical student, and added to this was the memory of his mother's final illness, which even through his old age never left him.

In fact, I believe it was this sorrow which motivated him to relentlessly force his ideas on the opposition which he faced from both Church and State later. Several of his siblings had suffered and died from tuberculosis, followed then by his father, and he had then to watch his mother, still a young woman, lie moaning in great pain, day by day, without priest or doctor calling to attend her suffering. In the very small town where she lived, they must have known the situation, particularly the important point to them — that she would be unable to pay the doctor, or offer money to the church. The same old state of affairs, 'Your money or your life' (even your afterlife!) continued as it had been for years before. Living in Newcastle about 1945, I remember a lady who looked after orphan children. She was poor, but gave love and attention to these children, making them happy by bringing them to the sea a couple of miles away, the five or six of them sitting on a cart drawn by her donkey. One of the boys who was handicapped died when about fourteen years of age. A good Christian woman, but poor, she was informed that the local church would not have a Mass said for this boy, because she couldn't pay for it.

This was the kind of injustice and suffering which Noel, and I am sure, many others, wished to see ended. Before this could happen, however, Noel believed that there would have to be changes made, one in particular being separation of Church and State; in his view, as in actual fact, the Church was not a democratically elected body, though it had a great hold over the people, whereas the State was democratically elected. The Church was there to care for the souls who wished to listen, not to care for their sick bodies; that was for doctors of medicine, though they (mainly consultants) eventually joined with the Church in defeating Noel's proposals in the end — worried about their pockets perhaps?

This was a difficult battle for Noel, but he never faltered, for he knew he had right on his side in the person of a well-qualified theologian who kindly guided him through the objections of the Roman Catholic Church, and particularly those of John Charles Mc Quaid,

Archbishop of Dublin. It was "contrary to Catholic moral teaching" the Church insisted — conveniently ignoring any obligation to 'social' teaching — for the State to interfere in family matters. To provide for one's children's health was the parent's right, even if it was sadly ludicrous to us to imagine the hundreds of very poor families living in the squalid conditions of the Dublin slums, being able to save money for a doctor, dentist, or even the greengrocer. Had the Hierarchy no idea of how their flock lived in the back streets? Had any one of them ever sat, waiting for medical attention, in a sordid dispensary where there were many destitute citizens, ill and hungry?

Still trying to finalise the matter satisfactorily, and without seeming to be uncooperative with either the Cabinet or the Hierarchy, Noel did all he was asked to do by Mr MacBride. This involved visiting the Bishops of various dioceses in the country, Galway, Cashel, as well as Cardinal Dalton of Armagh, Ferns, and of course the Archbishop of Dublin, Dr McQuaid. These visits, Noel knew, were a wanton squandering of his valuable time. He knew too that the forces against him were huge.

When these visits were over, and Noel reported their outcomes, every member of the Cabinet and the Clann na Poblachta Party was asked, one by one, whether they agreed with the Hierarchy — who of course had told Noel they were against his proposals. Naturally the Cabinet agreed with the Bishops, as did MacBride, the 'Republican', who demanded Noel's resignation, but did not succeed in breaking his spirit.

This proved the end of the saga, for within weeks there was a General Election. The general public, on the whole even more disgusted with the behaviour of their politicians, returned Noel. And the Catholic Church, for so long looked up to by the Irish people, was never again quite so powerful.

From now on, Noel's future in the Dáil was to be spent on the back benches. Many more matters needed to be improved, especially regarding social issues, such as the acceptance of homosexuality, contraception and divorce, inter- and non-denominational education, the truly, awful laws on corporal and capital punishment, and, even way back in the early Fifties, the dangers of smoking, which only recently, with reluctance, are now accepted. Advancing these changes with continual persistence, Noel knew it would take many years for them to come about; still fearful of the Roman Catholic Church, many TDs were slow to back Noel, afraid of "a belt of a crozier" as the blacksmith TD, General Sean McEoin admitted. One other fact of Irish life which he greatly wished to bring to the attention of the Government, was the inequality and general difficulties of our Irish womenfolk. At every possible opportunity he spoke out for them, either in the Dáil or in speeches organised by the women's movements. And I believe that many of them appreciated his interest in trying to better their lives, which even yet still need attention.

New Horizons,
Family Fortunes
&
Insane Deeds

Return to Medicine, 1951

Even though we felt a certain amount of disappointment at Noel's having to leave his Ministry with much more needing to be done, Noel was still in the Dáil, and could continue putting forward his ideas as an Independent TD. It was now possible to return to our old home, the lodge at the hospital gates, and get back to work for his patients. As Noel had taken unpaid leave of absence when he entered politics, there was no problem in this regard. Indeed we were pleased to return, our only problem being the age-old one: personal finance.

I am quite sure that many people believe that politicians, and indeed doctors, can make a lot of money, and indeed they can — most of them. In our case, it was during Noel's period as Minister that we got into serious debt. As a Minister, Noel actually earned less than his Departmental Secretary, and to help keep the expenses of the party offices, he was also expected to forfeit half of his salary to it. Added to these expenses was the purchase of a reliable car, which we never had owned, and the expenses of running it. Then we had to rent a house, one after another, for somehow it proved difficult to rent for longer than six months, possibly because few people believed the Government would last any longer than that length of time? At any rate, by the time we were back in the lodge, we were in the same situation, as far as finance was concerned, as when we had left it.

Nevertheless, we settled down happily, able to see a lot more of each other, and be less apprehensive. We could even find time, generally at weekends, when the Dáil would not be sitting, to enjoy occasional days together, swimming in the lakes, sitting under the refreshing pools of the mountain streams, and picnics on the sandy shore of Brittas Bay. Lighting a sweet smelling fire of timber in the woods of Aughavannagh, cooking a panful of sausages, and boiling a kettle for tea, was always Noel's speciality, giving our daughters an especially happy memory of their young days with their father.

Making Ends Meet

Though not yet at school, our daughters, now aged about five and seven years, were big enough and anxious enough to help me with my wish to try to contribute towards our household expenses. I felt I should do something to help out but what could I do? My domestic talents were all I had, such as they were.

Ruth suggested keeping hens, while Susan thought she would like rabbits. We decided to have both, the hens would supply us with eggs, while the rabbits, chinchillas, we would sell. Our garage was large enough to hold a hundred rabbits on one side, and a batch of one-day-old chicks on the other side, which were later moved over into a wooden hen-house where they quickly grew and began to lay. I went to market and bought four little pigs, whom we named Matthew, Mark, Luke and John. Noel made a crooked pigsty for them of concrete blocks. They grew so quickly that after a few months, they were able to jump over the wall of the sty and run across the lawn to the back door, snorting for more food. We were fond of the pigs, friendly clean animals, contrary to what most people think. They loved to lie down in their straw-lined sty, while I stroked them with a scrubbing brush, their eyes closed as a cat does when having its fur smoothed, stretched on the best cushion.

However, we made a mistake perhaps in being too friendly with our animals, especially the pigs, for when they realised they could jump over Noel's wall, they would come to our windows and look into the rooms, inquisitive as cats. They did precisely this, to my embarrassment, when an 'aristocratic' gentleman, who had been with Noel during his English public-school days, arrived to visit us. I made efforts to impress the man, but upon seeing the pigs, he didn't wait for Noel's return from the hospital; instead he departed, wondering no doubt how could Noel have got into such a crazy way of life. The rabbits meanwhile were great favourites as pets for children, who called from near and far to buy them. And the hens were wonderful layers, whose eggs I bartered for necessary groceries in our nearby little store. But the pigs I had to eventually part with, which I found upsetting. Being a 'city girl', I had not foreseen the inevitable, even though the kind butcher from our little town, knowing I was fond of my animals, used to collect them, the pigs and the beautiful table poultry I raised, early in the morning so that I would not hear the commotion the poor things naturally made. And he sold them always at a good price for me, to the nuns in a Bray boarding school.

Our domestic pets were part of the family, a Staffordshire bull terrier, a dachshund and a Siamese cat. Butchie, the bull terrier, was easily the most troublesome of all. He fought fiercely with every dog he met, and swam out to sea for miles after seagulls, so that we often had to rent a rowboat to fetch him before he got to Holyhead. It was a sort of madness he had. Once forgetting he was not on firm ground, but on a boat in Dun Laoghaire, he fell off the deck with the excitement of chasing the gulls, and sank right down to the bottom of the harbour. Wagging his tail with delight as we pulled him out, he splashed us all, then repeated the performance. Another time we actually lost him for two days. While picnicking in Brittas, he had swum out to sea as he usually did, but this time went so far that when it came time for our return home, he kept on swimming, unable to hear our anxious calls to him. We had to leave him reluctantly, meaning to return early next morning, when he was not to be seen. A phone call from a friend the following day, however, gave us the joyous news that he had found Butchie wandering by the sea. He knew the dog was ours and brought him home to us.

But the most mischievous thing Butchie ever did was to steal a leg of lamb. My mother and a few relations were coming to lunch, not long after we had moved back into the lodge. Our kitchen was really primitive — no cooker, just a tiny smoky range which wouldn't even burn turf. I cooked with great dexterity (until I eventually got a bad shock) on an electric cooking ring on the floor, placing one pot over another as necessary. On the particular day when my visitors were coming I decided to cook a leg of lamb, slowly, with vegetables. Leaving the kitchen for a short while, to clean up the house and light a fire, I returned to see how the cooking was faring. What greeted me? Butchie, tail wagging in thanks, walking around the kitchen with the leg of lamb in his big jaws. Too horrified to even scold him, I took it out of his mouth, ran the cold tap over it, tidied it up, and returned it to the pot. There was nothing else I could do, no time or money to go to the village for something else. Of course, I should have put the lid on the pot, I told myself, and not put such temptation in the dog's way — but I was so busy.

My visitors arrived, had their look around the house, then sat down to their lunch of lamb, vegetables and sauce, little knowing that my dog had already tasted it. To my great relief, on their leaving for home, none of them showed any sign of illness. Butchie really tried our patience. Ugly enough anyway, as that breed is, he was hardly ever without large black scars; or worse, after an especially serious fight, his head, when he shook it, rattled as though there were loose machinery parts in it! Our dachshund and Siamese gave no trouble, though they were looked upon by our local friends as being a little odd; one man assured me not to worry about the dog — "his legs will eventually grow" — and they'd never seen such a strange looking cat.

Though the rabbits were easily sold, the hens failed to help our finances sufficiently; as a local farmer often said to me, "A hen never died but in debt". Therefore I had to think of a more successful way to increase our bank balance — or imbalance. Eventually the best idea came. Why had I not thought of it before? It was so much more sensible to work at my sewing machine when the children were asleep, and before Noel got home from Dublin, where he was often either in the Dáil or a meeting until quite late.

So once a month, I would take the bus to Dublin, to find the best value I could in materials for evening wear. I had had practice in making dresses very quickly when I needed one to attend some evening event when Noel was Minister. Moreover, it was work which I had always enjoyed, and I silently thanked my mother for passing on her talent to me. Gradually I built up a small business, sewing garments for the hospital staff, even a uniform for a hospital matron, as well as confirmation and wedding dresses.

At about this time 'boutiques' were becoming fashionable, and, to my delight, I came across a pleasant business-like young girl who was anxious to open such a shop in Bray. This was the opportunity I had been wishing for, and within a few weeks a little shop, complete with several rails of attractive day and evening wear, was open. I earned reasonable prices for my work, and the dresses sold quickly. I had a few less worries then, like hurrying past shops I owed money to, always a hateful experience.

A Surprise for Noel

Still, it occurred to me that while I was happily busy every day with our daughters and their friends, Noel's life was passing by with little enjoyment — just the constant strain of his medical and political duties. Since leaving Dublin, we had eventually found a lot more time to be together; nevertheless Noel's working day was long, attending to his patients until late afternoon, then driving to Dublin if the Dáil was sitting. Knowing how, in years gone by, he always found solace in sailing, I thought it would be a wonderful idea if I could get him a sailing boat, something modest to help him get off the land, and to help him find peace and relief. Sailing must be one of the most gentle pastimes, just the natural forces of wind and water to contend with. And on the way home from the Dáil, or at weekends, he could drop by Dun Laoghaire harbour, to sail around the bay and return home refreshed.

I had read in the newspaper of a credit company in Dublin, and without mentioning my plan to Noel, I went along to a little office in Molesworth Street, where I asked a pleasant lady could I borrow to buy a boat? By this time, I was making enough money by my sewing to be able to tell the lady that I could pay back a little every month. She was delighted to help — "The first boat enquiry I've had," she said, "until now it's always been cars."

Noel found a beautiful old sailing boat in Castletownsend in Cork, which he sailed up to Dun Laoghaire, to enjoy many years' sailing with Ruth, Susan, Butchie of course, and many friends. It was a joy to us all to see how happy he was to get back on the sea.

With my sewing efforts, life was a little easier, though still not easy enough to save the amount needed to put towards a deposit for a house. We had decided that it would be wiser to try to have our own house, rather than stay on in the lodge, for there might come a day, we thought, when the hospital would close, with the possibility of there being only a few patients, in time.

Delivering my gowns to the boutique one day, I noticed a little shop preparing to open up as a delicatessen. After a chat, the pleasant owner agreed to take my cakes on trial. Cooking has always been a pleasure to me, so it took no time to reach an agreement. I was to supply as many cakes as possible every day, for a fair price. This was a successful venture for quite some time until, unfortunately, the owner decided to move to larger premises, too far away for me. And I believe he is still in business in the West of Ireland.

While I was busy at my various interests, Noel, if not sailing, enjoyed trying to make his contributions. With the children's help, he would make toothpaste, which looked good, but was most unpleasant and unusable due to the undisguised taste of bread soda. He also made lavender water, for there was plenty of this beautiful plant growing nearby, but this too, while looking good, had little scent, more water than lavender. And to the delight of the children, he also made orange squash, which tasted good, and was harmless. Another time we bought sacks of apples suitable for making cider. Putting them into a large bath, we did as the cider factories do — we thought — and, as the apples became softer and softer, we stamped on them in our bare feet to make the juices come out. In time, we put this juice into bottles, and, after leaving it for a week to settle, were delighted with the taste. We sampled it every Sunday morning, until, finally, we considered it to be perfect. However, spilling her glass by accident in the garden, Sue noticed that the grass immediately became brown, as though burnt. We drank no more of Noel's cider, nor did the grass ever become green again.

A House of Our Own, 1952

Kept busy cooking, sewing, and enjoying the children's various pleasures during the day, I would look around with Noel at houses for sale in the evenings. Every auctioneer in the town of Bray had a visit from me from time to time, until, at last, a suitable house came on the market; indeed it was more than suitable, it was just perfect for us, and we would have wished to live there forever if possible. And the price was so low that even our offer was acceptable.

Previously a holiday home for deprived city children, it was set back from the road by a pretty lavender-edged path. With the bank's help, we happily moved in. Unlived in for some years, the damp had decorated the walls with attractive verdigris, climbing fern-shapes. With many large tins of paint, all brightly coloured, along with rolls of wallpaper and yards of flowery curtaining, I set to work and in time the house was an attractive home, perfect for the children and their friends, as there were so many rooms.

With the discovery of furniture auctions in Bray, I was able to buy Victorian pieces, which people were getting rid of, replacing them with light veneered furniture. Having lived in a furnished house owned by the hospital, we had nothing of our own, except a few hens and their hen house, and the dogs and cats. A helpful man who worked for the auctioneer offered to carry these sole belongings on his horse and cart. With the hens clacking and the dogs barking, we journeyed down the main street towards our new home. The good people of Bray, then a smaller town than now, no doubt thought, "Here come the gypsies", for the children, their friends and I had to walk beside the horse and cart, so that the animals would not become troublesome until we reached the house.

Acquiring the necessary household articles by degrees at auctions, we eventually settled down again, happier than ever. In time the house became a pretty home, the old furniture upholstered in different colours of velvet. After a few attempts, I found this quite easy to do. Along with cheap and cheerful carpeting, Ruth's artistic efforts on the walls made such a difference.

A large fruit garden and plenty of grass and outhouses, plus a flat roof, reached by wooden stairs from the garden, meant happy days for all the young, who even slept on it under the stars. I would leave a tray, breakfast and flasks of tea for them, before I myself went to bed. I suspect however a picnic was held long before breakfast time.

What a pity, I often thought, that Noel could not share in at least some of all this happiness the children and their friends enjoyed. Few people realise the toll which can be suffered in a family when the father works anti-social hours, such as politicians must. He is lost to them from morning to night every day, resulting in almost a one-parent family. Sailing was, of course, always a help to get us all together, but the wind and the tide must be right, to go out to the bay.

In order that Noel did not feel too cut off from our daughter's various interests, I never went to bed until he returned home, sometimes after midnight if he had to travel a distance from a political meeting. I liked those quiet hours when we could talk over his day's work, and any problems or stories, as well as in later years, the children's school difficulties or accomplishments. Even at that late hour Noel would enjoy a meal, for he disliked eating out. This habit did not worry me, as there was nothing I would refuse to do to keep him well, he was so precious to us all. Cooking at 2 a.m. was all right with me.

So that the children would never feel that he had left them, he always brought home two chocolate biscuits, to put under their pillows as they slept. For a long time, Susan believed that the Custom House (which housed the Department of Health) was a chocolate biscuit factory!

Education

We were slower than most parents we knew in sending Ruth and Sue to school, as I consider it cruelty to send a child of three or four years of age to even the most expensively furnished school with plenty of toys, books, and paints. Not only is it unnatural for a mother to hand over her child to a teacher whom she may have no reason to trust, but, more importantly, the child needs the loving company and understanding of its mother, which no one else can replace. This was also when teachers were allowed to punish their pupils for any misdemeanour, and the children's friends had horrific stories to tell about how they were treated in the local convent.

A child can learn so much at home, merely by questioning, conversing with its parents, by experimenting and, as Ruth and Susan did, by learning simple songs and dancing regularly to my piano playing before bedtime. Noel taught them about gardening and I remember how on one Christmas Day they made a fine rockery in the front of the house. Giving them rides in his wheelbarrow helped to make it fun for them, and to look after their growing plants became an interest for them. Thus we felt they need not hurry into formal education, and indeed they could read before they went to school.

With luck we eventually heard of a small school in the town of Bray. It was just big enough for twenty pupils, each treated as individuals by a patient lady. It was perfect for children starting their education, no fear whatever, no worries about keeping up with each other, just trying their best and being praised for trying as each child worked at their own pace.

Ruth, when she reached the higher classes learned shorthand and typing in her spare time between her usual subjects. An artistic and musical child, she eventually passed all the necessary examinations needed for the teaching of piano and art. Her talents have been a help to her, and to our joy, she has passed them on to her daughter, who plays the flute. Susan, a more outgoing person, preferring to work with people, enjoyed office duties in a hospital in Dublin after leaving school. We would have liked to have been able to send them to university, but for obvious reasons this was impossible. Yet they grew up to be intellectually bright, independent and practical, caring and thoughtful young people, and always understanding of Noel's ways and work.

We did try various convents when the school in Bray could no longer take them after fourteen years of age. It was an interesting exercise. After a short time the nuns would treat them as though they were lapsed Catholics. "Stand up those girls whose parents are of mixed religions," the nuns would say, and our girls would be the only ones. Meanwhile the Protestant schools would not consider taking them at all. "The sins of the father fell upon the children", as the Protestants thought they were too 'Catholic'. I suppose for the same 'sins', we were refused our application to adopt an orphan child. We knew there were a good number of such children, looked after by the nuns, and we chose a little coloured girl, but when it came to the final arrangements, we were refused, without a reason.

Before marrying Noel, for some reason I had to go to the local priest for "instruction" on the "Ne Temere" Decree. Against my better judgement, I visited this gentleman at ten o'clock on Monday mornings. Waiting in his room, I noticed signs of a party having been held the night before, whisky bottles, glasses, playing cards. No real harm in that I suppose, but I gave up my visits nevertheless, and never signed the paper.

Doctor Seeks Employment

During all these years after we left the hospital lodge, Noel was still working as before, driving the ten or so miles to the hospital every day, then returning to go on to Dublin if the Dáil was sitting, a total of at least fifty miles a day altogether, each way. With Ruth and Susan following their various interests, we were enjoying life in our old house, but our luck was running out. We had foreseen that the hospital would close, perhaps within a few years, but the blow came sooner than expected, in December, 1963.

Tuberculosis had been beaten, the beds no longer needed, which of course was wonderful news — except that we were now unemployed. Noel's speciality was tuberculosis: now what were we to do? General practice he ruled out, as he disliked to ask a sick person for payment, preferring to earn a salary from the State, where no matter how many patients, or how ill they were, he would earn the same amount every month. I remember a time when in Newcastle hospital, a junior doctor became ill and asked Noel to take over his once-a-week clinic in Harcourt Street, where Dublin patients would go for whatever medical attention they needed, rather than travel down to Newcastle, a tiring and expensive journey by bus. When patients turned up, Noel gave them whatever medicine or attention they needed; then, as was their custom with the junior doctor, they would ask "What do I owe you for that, Doctor?" "There's a plate on the hall table, leave whatever you wish, or nothing, on it" was Noel's reply. Nothing was ever left on it, much to Noel's relief, but I admit that on his return home from those few weeks in Harcourt Street, I was a little disappointed.

That was long ago, however, whereas now life was more serious. We talked over our problem with our daughters, who, like ourselves, had no wish whatever to emigrate, as so many unfortunate people had to during those years. Between 1950–60, around 1,000 people left Ireland every week, I believe.

The only answer left for us now was for Noel to start another branch of medicine, psychiatry, the only State-run service at the time. But before this could be achieved, Noel would have to return to university and study until qualified. We all agreed on this, as there was no alternative, though we knew we faced more problems — leaving the home we were so fond of, being one. By now it was attractive, and comfortable, but we would have to give it up to have a little money. It did not take long before a buyer came along, but where were we to live now, having made very little profit on the sale? We all loved 'Tumbledown', as it was called by some of the children's friends, and we knew we'd never find another like it, certainly not for the price we had paid for it — £800!

Moving house can be a traumatic experience, as one also has to leave one's neighbours, the local shops one has become used to, the familiar Church bells, favourite public houses, and much, much more. Our neighbours were particularly friendly and helpful, and the local children were unusually amusing, for they had a trick of climbing our high back wall, collecting any fruit which happened to be in season, apples for instance, then knocking at the front door, asking did I wish to buy them? So I bought my own apples! Another trick they had was to fill a sack with timber they found in one of our outhouses, then to the front door, as with the apples, offering the timber at a 'reduced price'. I liked talking to these children, and was interested to notice that, in time, they realised this sort of 'fun', if they continued it, would eventually get them into trouble. A year later, after our move to our next home, I met them in Bray town, where they were proud of being able to tell me they were working — 'all crimes are crimes of society'!

Having to leave our home left us nearer to desperation than we had ever felt before, including our years in politics, and Noel's illnesses. It was going to be such an upset for our daughters, and my little businesses of sewing and cooking would have to be forgotten also, for it was certain that whatever house we could find, and could afford, would be outside the town, where property cost less. However the deed had to be done. The bank, hearing that the hospital was going to close, insisted on our repaying the small loan which we had been given by them. With profits of millions, banks cannot afford to lose a few hundred pounds.

Seeing an advertisement in the local newspaper of the forthcoming auction of a condemned school, a few miles further into the country from Bray, I went along to see what condition the building was in. Built of granite, about 60' by 40', it was typical of a school of the last century, with small high windows, so that the pupils would not waste their time looking out, and absolutely no facilities for washing, though I did notice outside taps.

The auction day arrived, and, with no enthusiasm whatever, I made up my mind that I had no choice but to go to it. Half-a-dozen local country women were standing around, waiting for the auctioneer; chatting while leaning on the iron entrance gates, they were obviously there just to pass the time, not to buy. I was not at all impressed by the building, there was simply no poetry about it, but life at this stage had become serious for us, and even if there were good reasons for the school having been condemned, I had to get it, if at all possible. At least it had a roof — but was it rain proof?

The auctioneer arrived, and hurriedly asked for his first bid. Complete silence, until I found the courage to say £200. Probably stunned by this ridiculous offer, even though it was the only one, he asked impatiently "Does no one want this fine building?" No, nobody did want it, yet he would not let it go.

After a few minutes' silence, as the women had stopped their murmurings, I bid £300, in a nervous, even quieter voice, wondering at the back of my mind at the same time where would I find that sum? To my great relief, the auctioneer, perhaps realising he was beaten, with no hopes of selling the school to anyone except me for any more than £300, said smiling at me, "It's all yours, and good luck." He did not even ask for his fee — it was worth so little to him I expect. The luck he wished was greatly needed, if I had only known.

I went home to report progress, where we were all feeling heavy-hearted, yet relieved that we now had somewhere to shelter. There was little else one could say for the old school. Our first hurdle meanwhile was to get the packing and moving over. If we had known of the trouble facing us for the next few months, we would have felt even more down-hearted. Our neighbours, the Costelloes, farmers who owned a large lorry for their animals, kindly offered to help and with their large family we filled it up to the top with our bits and pieces.

Off we set on yet another move, definitely downwards. The old school, even though only about eight miles away from the home we were leaving, might as well have been on the moon as far as we were concerned. No transport passed by for Ruth and Susan to get to their schools and meet their friends, but worse still, no water came out of the taps. The mains water did not pass by the school in the usual way by the roadside. Before going to the hospital, which had not yet closed, Noel would have to drive our old VW to the village, three hilly miles away, to fill a few barrels with water, and tow them home on a trailer for the day's supply. Eventually a well had to be drilled, by enormous noisy machines, working around the building for three weeks, and making the garden-to-be muddy and wet. None of us had ever before endured quite such hard physical work; even our daughters did a great amount to help, pushing and pulling 84-feet-long pipes down through the soil, painting walls and making valiant efforts at prettifying their little bedrooms. It took weeks before our school looked anything like a home, but we were very proud of our work when it was finished. Electricity brought the water in, Noel made magnificent fireplaces of stones which had fallen, through neglect, off walls of a nearby estate. In an old garage he found an attractive spiral staircase which the owner was willing to sell, and in junk yards in Dublin he found fine big windows to replace the originals. By this time we felt as perhaps the builders of the pyramids might have, by the time they got to the top! Poor Sue felt it was all too much, and decided to join her best friend at boarding school. But after a few weeks, she was home again with appendix trouble. In hospital for the necessary operation, she woke up from her anaesthetic to see a picture in *The Irish Times* of her father being bitten by an Alsatian dog, aided by the Gardaí. We quickly visited her to reassure her that Noel was not badly hurt and to explain to her how it happened.

Kruschev had missiles sent to Cuba to aid that country, threatened by a US invasion in an effort to abort Cuba's socialist revolution. Noel and his left-wing friends decided at a meeting they were attending that they had to make some protest by marching on the US Embassy in Ballsbridge. But violence broke out along the way, some of it by Gardaí. Savage Alsatians arrived in a police van, and were let loose when the protesters were near Clare Street. These angry, sharp-toothed animals tore at Noel, who was luckily wearing a thick coat and jacket, so he came out more disgusted than injured. While some of the young men and women needed hospital treatment, Noel treated his own wounds when he got home.

Another march was held, led by the writer Frank O'Connor, who was anxious to establish without question a citizen's right to march anywhere. This time, however, the police were not allowed to use Alsatians to disrupt the march.

Neither Ruth nor Sue took an active part in politics, and who could blame them? But they were always very aware of how society should be run, and through their friendships and work, showed, in the best way they could, how to act accordingly. Noel and I had treated them always as adults, though accepting and enjoying their childlike ways. They called us by our first names, never 'Mam and Dad', and gave their point of view on any subject, often spiced with the humour and insight inherited from Noel.

Mature Studenthood

We had known that the hospital would be closing down sometime, but, when the decision was made, and Noel advised of the definite date, it was earlier than we had expected, and, despite having been warned, we felt shocked and worried. Noel was now about fifty years of age, and it would not be easy for him to settle down to study, especially with so much else on his mind. Moreover, he was still in the Dáil.

For some time, Noel had been studying books on psychiatry, even while we were moving to the school, and he had remained working in the hospital, where there were still a few patients. Now, however, he could start serious study at the university, hoping in time to qualify and work in the new branch of medicine he had chosen.

Attending lectures at UCD and studying at home, with his usual tenacity, Noel eventually passed his examinations, gaining his DPM. With sighs of relief we could relax again and look forward to an easier life — we thought. At home, we thought it a wonderful effort on Noel's part to get through his examinations, and so we had a little celebration dinner for him. Susan was always an excellent cook, still is, and we bought a bottle of his favourite wine; in good times he loved wine with his meal in the evening — but that was not too often. Ruth too loves to cook, but the piano always called her when the washing-up was to be done!

Psychiatrist Needing Employment (Urgently), 1966

Hoping, even expecting that some city hospital would employ him, even starting at the bottom of the ladder, we found no helpful offers were forthcoming. "I could have you taken into a good place in England" was however one of many such suggestions. Indeed we felt we were being chased out of our own country. It seemed that the clerical/medical disapproval of Noel's political beliefs was continuing. The lingering dislike of his ideas, except with the general public, was still being used against him by those in authority. We had thought that this part of the battle was over, all the while wishing for some luck to keep us together with some future and hope. Without any feelings of self-pity, we felt we were on the edge of a cliff, where without warning, a wind would come some day, and blow us over into a rough sea.

Always aware that many families had to live very much harder lives than ours, we had in fact chosen what we wished to do with our lives, and had brought most of our woes upon ourselves. "A clear conscience fears no accusations", we told ourselves, knowing we had tried our best. Noel did as he knew he should have done, at some risk, and the experiences which we shared, with the help and understanding of our daughters, had been of benefit to each of us. To have so bravely used his young life's difficult years, continuing on through his later serious illnesses, shows us just how one person's dedication and commitment can be used to benefit less fortunate people, though of course he had help from many friends, like ships which passed in the night.

Now, however, we were about to start on yet another new life. Happily, after many visits to psychiatric hospitals and applications for a place, even the most menial, Noel called to Dr Dunne, head doctor of St Brendan's Hospital, the largest psychiatric hospital in the country. As Minister, Noel had met this doctor in connection with the improvement of the hospital and services, so it was with amusement and kindly help this gentleman now offered Noel the opportunity to start work in St Brendan's, though on the bottom rung of the ladder. So delighted with this news was Noel that he rang us at home from the first phonebox he could find, to give us the good news. Though he could have looked upon his new situation as stepping down the ladder from a Minister of State to teaboy, this would not have occurred to Noel, nor would the pay have mattered, which of course was pitiful!

Practising Psychiatry

As with every new interest he took up, as a qualified psychiatrist now, Noel had his own ideas for patients. He did not believe in keeping them indoors, under lock and key. Rather, by acquiring a mini-bus, he arranged to have them mix in the outside world, scheduling trips to the seaside for those well enough, along with visits to the theatre, and race meetings. Noel found the work most interesting, especially with the young boys and girls who had got into the drug scene. His patience with them was inexhaustible, for he looked upon them not as bad children, but disturbed, unhappy, unwanted, and unloved young people. For various reasons, such as having no parents, or some awful trauma, many of them had little hopes of ever being happy people.

I suggested to Noel that it might help make their lives more tolerable if they could visit me for an afternoon for tea and a chat. Few of them would have had any experience of home life, and so they were pleased to occasionally visit me. Most of their visits were trouble free, but a few were not.

One girl in particular I remember, as I was not at home to receive her. In anger, she pulled all our beautiful geraniums off the front of our house wall, strewing them along some twenty yards of the public road. Then, to rest herself after this exertion, she visited a little local teashop, where she ordered tea, cakes, and ice cream, "To be charged to Mrs Browne!" The kind proprietors knew me and agreed.

Part of Noel's duties was attending to the problems of the good people, mostly mothers and children, of the flats in Ballymun. It took him no time to realise that, like my teas, he was merely making ripples, and his efforts could be of no great value to the troubled families. Their problems were of such horrendous proportions, especially for the mothers in the high-rise flats looking after several children. He was at a loss as to how he could help, for instance, a lady with four children whose husband was unemployed or perhaps violent, or the family of six living in a flat meant for two. No gardens either for the children to play in safety, if the mother was living three or four storeys upstairs, looking after one or more small children. Contraception at this time would not be contemplated by Roman Catholic couples.

Today the fact that the Ballymun flats were a mistake has been acknowledged, and they are to be demolished. But well before this decision was made, Noel had concluded that the only hope of improving conditions for the tenants was to continually draw attention to their situation in the Dáil — where he was still working — the only place, cumbersome though the system is, where changes can be made.

A Year in Connemara, 1969

Perhaps Noel was not a suitable person to be a psychiatrist, for he became too involved with each patient's problem, and felt for them. Whereas one of the doctors in St Brendan's at some function told Noel of how he left the hospital every afternoon at five o'clock, no matter who or what needed him, and went off to play his game of golf. "Noel should do the same," the doctor advised.

The golf-playing doctor was correct, and eventually Noel felt compelled to ask for twelve-months leave of absence without pay, as a relief from the frustrating work in St Brendan's. He believed he was treating patients from 'the wrong end of the stick', and even Noel didn't believe he could change this procedure! Thus we would live as best we could for a year on our Dáil salary.

By this time our daughters could look after themselves, Susan having married a doctor she met while working in the Meath Hospital, and Ruth, now qualified to teach art and piano, was busy with pupils, and running her own life. So we were free for a year, a wonderful feeling. When Minister, Noel had travelled to Connemara during any free weekend he had, to learn to speak Irish. He remembered a little of the language from being at school, but, in order to answer questions put to him in Irish during question time in the Dáil, he had wished to become more fluent. By staying in the home of Sean Ó Conghaile in Connemara, and taking short lessons after his work in the Custom House, he soon became a fluent speaker.

Now introduced to Connemara, we became convinced, without any doubt, that this part of the earth was where we wished to live — to the end of our days if possible. For now, however, we had a year, during which we would search for a stone cottage and work on it to make it ready for the big day we could retire altogether.

Even in the late-Sixties we felt young and strong enough to face such a programme. It is so easy, when one feels fit, to forget that we are mere mortals, and death or illness is no respecter even of persons who might have a spirit of adventure. Moreover, Noel had already lived through five bouts of serious tuberculosis since our marriage and had yet to survive two heart attacks.

But one puts these cheerless thoughts at the back of one's mind, thankful that one *is*, and continues to make plans. And this latest plan was one of our best. We did, eventually, find an old unlived-in cottage, about four hundred years old, we were told, facing the fierce Atlantic ocean, with the three islands of Aran, lolling like big lazy old animals, across the sound. Not a sign of life between us and the islands except a few red cows, and occasionally a man and his dog looking after sheep, walking through the tiny fields, strangely called 'gardens', each surrounded by stone walls, even if they were only the size of the smallest front garden in the city.

There can be nowhere, anywhere, quite like Connemara. There one lives on the edge of the world, seeing the moon starting on its journey travelling through the stars at night. One sees the sun starting on its journey — first through gold-lined clouds, clouds which by evening might be racing towards one like a grey suited ogre ready for battle. Seldom does a day pass without a few changes in the weather, sun quickly followed by savage showers, and always, always a wind.

With neighbours, the weather is a constant talking point, quite often the only one. The wonder is that one can see it happening, no matter from what quarter it comes, and it's very seldom that one cannot also hear it, whistling through the walls or, in a really bad storm, sounding like a battering ram. One feels that the world is behind us, only the sea, sun, moon and stars before us, as all nature, except human nature, performs for us.

Without the help of good neighbours, however, we could never have made the cottage fit to live in. It had been used as a shelter for animals, and was still littered with straw and hay. Its roof was also starting to fall in, and needed rethatching. As for the stonework, even the quite young local boys seemed to have the natural talent needed with stone — I expect because their ancestors had worked with it for centuries — and they did wonderful work.

Thus within our year, the cottage was alive again, just as we ourselves had recovered from the stresses of city life from which we had fled. We fetched our water from a spring well, and lived by candles, until, in time, we had gaslight installed. Several years went by until, in the early Seventies, electricity and telephone services arrived. We really preferred the old ways, but had to be practical. One thing we did keep however was the open fire for cooking and heat. Food cooked in the old black pots and griddles always tasted better than by any modern method. On the roadside between Dublin and Galway we came across groups of 'travelling people' who always had a line of old-time wares for sale, and it was from their collection we bought, very cheaply, old cooking utensils and many prettily flowered milk jugs for the old-fashioned dresser.

It took many years, perhaps ten, before the cottage was fit to inhabit with some sort of comfort. We came down during holidays, and weekends, laden with kitchen sinks, pipes, paint, and worked hard making improvements. We wanted to make it as perfect as we could, ready for the day we would return for the remainder of our lives.

However, for the present, alas, our year's freedom was over and reluctantly we returned to the city, quite convinced that we would be back within a few years, but dismayed at the thoughts of not hearing the sounds and seeing the sights we had become accustomed to in such a short time.

But did we really have to leave? The answer, we knew, was yes — there was unfinished business waiting in Dublin. We had had occasional feelings of guilt during our year away, even though throughout the year Noel had travelled to Dublin to attend to his duties in the Dáil, and his constituency. It would be pleasant to see our daughters again too, though they had visited us from time to time.

Noel still had ideas he wanted to try to carry through, particularly with regard to improving the lives of women, whom he always considered to be treated as second-class citizens, with few civil rights such as divorce. He was also working with a wonderful lady, Nancy Hatte, who was trying to stop the cruel export of horses at this time. This proved a successful venture, which passed through the Dáil and greatly pleased Noel who would not kill a spider or a fly. Even a mouse found in the bath one morning was gently caught and put out into the garden!

Return to Dublin, 1970

Sometimes we wondered were we a little childish in our behaviour? For two intelligent people, we did not seem to be able to accept the sort of regular life most of our friends lived! Instead we opted for the more unsettled lifestyle that Noel's career demanded and, difficult as it was at times, this was how we wished to make our contribution, small as it might be, in making life more tolerable for others.

So, we returned to our old schoolhouse home, much improved since we had left it, for Ruth had planted trees, shrubs, hedges and flowers around the garden, giving the house a pretty 'cottage' appearance. Inside too, it was cosy, and furnished with Ruth's painting's and her good, though simple, taste.

After finalising arrangements with the doctors, Noel returned to his psychiatric work in St Brendan's Hospital, knowing well there was little he could do to help the patients, while at the same time working in the Dáil. On our return to Dublin, nothing had changed on either the medical or political fronts — that is, nothing that made any difference to the man in the street. Was it Daniel O'Connell who responded, when a labouring Kerry man asked him how he would be affected if O'Connell was successful, "No matter what happens, you'll still be breaking stones." It does seem true that big bodies move slowly, and it takes something drastic to happen if the ordinary citizen's life is to be improved. Still, endless political meetings in smoky halls and basements were held by Noel and his like-minded friends, trying to get the many left-wing splinter groups to join together, but no agreement could be reached. Noel felt as though he was a frustrated watchdog, just howling into the wind.

Meanwhile, two small incidents happened that made me think to myself that he should think of giving up, and settle for medicine only. Apart from the frightening fact that he suffered a heart attack while driving from the hospital to the Dáil in the city, and was hospitalised for a few weeks, I heard a story from one of his friends which told me that he was becoming either very tired, or simply losing heart. After leaving a meeting late one night, he walked along the quays talking to a friend. Having not eaten all day, he bought an orange in a nearby shop, peeled it, and most unlike him, went to throw the peel into the river. But instead of throwing in the peel, he threw in his car keys, which he was holding in his other hand. However, after great difficulty, a clever mechanic friend got the car to start.

The second incident which worried me was finding him on the wrong platform in Dun Laoghaire Station. Instead of waiting for the train to Bray, he was on the platform for Dublin. Of course, I always knew he was easily 'lost', perhaps because he had a lot on his mind. Once, in London, a taxi left him at a certain hotel. Having settled into his room and unpacked, he went for a walk. His walk turned out to be far longer than he intended, for he couldn't remember the name of the hotel he was staying in. Round and round the streets of London he walked, but they all looked the same. Eventually of course, something small, a certain kind of door handle perhaps, helped him to remember where he was staying!

However, no suggestion or hint to slow up was taken notice of. Nothing, just nothing, would ever allow Noel to give up, or even slow up in his work. It was not his nature. No matter what the task, be it cooking a meal, mending a puncture, explaining a problem to our grandchildren, or particularly of course, attending to his patients, there was always his enduring passion to get the task done quickly and perfectly. It was as if a flash of lightning possessed him, giving him energy.

Unlike most men, Noel never made any deep friendships with his colleagues. When the day's work was over in the Dáil, generally by ten o'clock, the majority of TDs would retire to the bar for refreshment and, no doubt, gossip. But Noel would return home immediately, as our time together was always precious, and we wished not to waste any of it. We had of course many friends, people we admired and enjoyed conversations with in our home. Of these friends there was a family in Dun Laoghaire, the father a great sailor who spent many hours sailing with Noel. Late one night this man phoned us in great excitement, asking Noel to go to his home immediately, as his wife was giving birth to twins. Never having practised obstetrics in the usual way, though he had passed through the necessary course in the Rotunda Hospital, Noel disliked having to do anything with actual birth, and avoided attending them since he had become qualified.

Yet this request from his friend was something he could not refuse. After a little hesitation, he got out of bed, and rushed off to help his friend as best he could. After an hour he returned home with the news that the twins had safely arrived, though he could hardly speak about his experience. After a hot whiskey, he returned to bed and slept soundly, but never again spoke of that night.

For many years we visited this family on occasion, watching with interest how the twins were growing. In time, knowing that the parents were not married, Noel thought that for the sake of the children's future — passports and marriage certificates which they might need — it might be wise for the parents to arrange to do so. Also, the father was quite elderly, and if he died, the mother would have little money to keep her children in comfort and education.

Eventually, they agreed to marry, though the father showed a little reluctance. The service was arranged with the local priest, to be performed in late evening when the church would likely be empty. The lady, having sent her twins to the cinema for the evening, arrived first. For an anxious half-hour the three of us waited for the father to show up, but there was no sign of him. In desperation Noel walked the length of the town in search of the reluctant bridegroom, and eventually found him. He had been looking for another church — the wrong one — and was standing at the corner studying a flock of birds! (Interested in birds, and indeed all animals, he even kept a gibbon monkey in his house, allowing it to jump around the rooms as it wished, always looking for bananas.) With Noel as their witness, the pair of them went into the right church, where the ceremony was carried out by the impatient priest.

Glad to have got the service over, we walked down to a nearby public house to celebrate, the bride's best friend and her husband joining us. In the usual fashion the men huddled together, while we three ladies sat apart at our own table, myself thinking that this was an even more bizarre wedding than our own! The bride and her friend spent their time discussing how they would bury their menfolk when the time came. The friend would have hers put into a steel box and brought out in a friend's boat to be dumped at the Kish lighthouse, "where he could roll around as long as he liked", while the bride, decided cremation would be her choice. The ashes she would put on their mantelpiece, just so she would not forget him completely, "safely enclosed in an egg timer, which the twins could play with"!

No doubt the children enjoyed their film that night, but for all the arrangements made for their and their mother's future welfare, it was she who died first, and the father who lived with his twins for many more years, 'happy as a sandman'. This sort of outcome would make you wonder! In any case it was certainly the most unusual medical-cum-wedding case Noel ever had to deal with.

Slowing Down, The 1970s

During the Seventies Noel was becoming more and more disillusioned, as he felt there was a sort of stagnation within politics in the country. In 1972 he was appointed as a consultant psychiatrist to the Eastern Health Board. Working in a mental hospital, however, gave him very little, if any, satisfaction because the results of his work were of such little value to the patients.

Looking back on our lives since we became interested in politics, there was no doubt that some improvements had taken place in Ireland, even though slowly. The simple chance of survival is now greater since the days of large families such as mine and Noel's, and education and general living standards are higher, though too many still live in wretched houses: hungry, unemployed and uneducated.

Our country is also a little less sectarian, a little more tolerant. I doubt, for example that any politician today would dare pass a remark such as Sean MacBride once did to Noel. The occasion was the opening of a new wing for sick children at the Rotunda Hospital in the early Fifties, when Noel was Minister. A photograph appeared in the newspaper next day, with Noel standing beside the Protestant Archbishop of Dublin. "You should not have allowed yourself to be photographed with the Protestant Archbishop," was MacBride's rebuke.

The power of the Roman Catholic Church, which they enjoyed for very many years, is now less obvious. Who would credit that, at one time, a cleric would interfere in the buying of a house in which we were interested. Yet a Bray priest stopped the sale, simply ordered the owner not to sell to us. Another time a solicitor tried to prevent us from renting a house in Malahide in the early 70s. "You're not allowing those people to rent your house?" was the solicitor's remark to the owner, who luckily ignored this advice! We even had a sale stopped once because the potential buyers discovered that a person with tuberculosis had once lived in it — Noel himself. From a financial point of view, this was a disastrous event for us at that time, but it shows how things were then.

Meanwhile, our minds were still considering our plan made several years before, of returning to our little cottage. Neither of us, strangely, mentioned a desire to do so, but somehow we both knew it was coming nearer as a sensible idea. But political life was to continue for Noel for some years, both as a Senator and subsequently a TD for Dublin North–Central, a seat he held until he retired in 1981. In the years immediately following our return from Connemara we moved to a beautiful home in Malahide, rented to us for a reasonable sum by a very kind local lady, Mrs Chadwick. We had been turned down for accommodation many times for reasons I could never fully understand — perhaps political — so we were grateful for this opportunity to live in this Victorian cottage with its magnificent gardens — roses around the door, filled with shrubs and trees, flowers and fruit — an array of lilac, orange blossom, lavender and roses. We passed ten happy years there, on free evenings often taking the short drive to Howth to walk along the pier, or even Howth Head, ending with a drink in the local public house, before returning to our cosy fireside.

The Connemara move to a life of peace and quiet was still a few years away, however. First, meanwhile, was another move into the countryside — though not necessarily a move to peace and quiet — when in the mid-1970s we decided to take up farming on Djouce Mountain in Wicklow, blissfully unaware of what lay ahead!

An Amateur Farmer's
Journal

More than most couples we knew, we had had our share of surprises, good and bad, while our friends appeared to live 'normal' lives, work 'normal' hours, and seldom change their address. I often wondered were they bored? Certainly that was a feeling we never experienced, least of all during the following episode of our life together. Noel, along with all the staff of the closed-down sanatorium, had received a lump sum from the Government as redundancy payment. What excitement! It was not a large amount, but it permitted us to buy a small property — the first acres we had ever owned — as well as pay our debts, and breathe easy for a little while.

Without hesitation — no banks or moneylenders of any kind needed — we chose a little lodge on twenty acres of Djouce Mountain in Co Wicklow. Noel always believed that if one had money, one should invest it in property, but then he was a man who always felt he had money, or would be lucky enough some day to inherit some, though from whom he never could tell. Anyway, this is what we did. I should have known better — that any property should be in a reasonably 'sensible' location, not at the top of a mountain, reached by driving through three large fields, all needing their gates to be opened and closed on the way into the house and out!

But I did like the place very much. It was a genuine Georgian lodge, once used by the local Lord, when hunting, to stop by and refresh his company and his animals. Hidden by trees and hedges, it was far from the road; the only sounds coming to the house were those of the river running by and the wind in the trees: sounds like the sea.

Within a week or two, we had the land stocked with sheep, pigs, hens, cows, and five beautiful Connemara ponies. Selling all these in the local market was to finance us. Also, for the first time in my life I had a car, an old Morris Minor, so that I could look after the needs of the animals and ourselves. In our innocence we were beginning to feel as though we were real farmers. Noel, in his usual frantic way, in a hurry to try everything, loved the life, especially the ponies which he schooled. From 7 a.m. to nightfall we were constantly on the move, seeing that all animals were fed and cleaned before we got to rest. Water for the house and the farmyard was brought up by electricity from a nearby river, but we could never enjoy a bath, although there was endless water. We could always fill the bath with good warm water, and get into it to soothe our weary bones. But for some reason, condensation problems no doubt, the ceiling always dripped cold, cold drops, so that we actually lay back in the bath holding an open umbrella for shelter! This was the only drawback in the house, but an uncomfortable one.

The morning after the sheep arrived, we leaned on the gate looking into them, wondering why they were still sitting quietly. We knew they would have been tired after their long journey from Wicklow Town, but surely they would have also been hungry, and there was plenty of good grass to tempt them. Deciding to inspect them closely, we walked into the field, whereupon they hardly moved. Upon opening the mouths of a few sheep, however, we knew what was wrong and our hearts sank.

The animals were ancient, toothless, useless, and had to be got rid of, at some loss.

As for the hens, I had had plenty of experience with them in the lodge at the hospital, and I was sure that at least we would always have fresh eggs. But clever foxes and the damage they do had not entered my head, until gradually my poor hens disappeared. There was no way I could prevent the foxes coming down from the forest behind us, day or night.

Disappointed with the loss of our sheep and hens so soon, I went off to the local mart intending to get a few more pigs and perhaps a cow or two, while Noel stayed behind with the ponies. There was already a good outhouse, ready for a few pigs, and therefore no need for Noel's building talent which he had used at the hospital lodge — all crooked walls, and not high enough!

At the mart, every farmer seemed to have his own signal to let the auctioneer know which animal he wanted, and how much he'd pay for it. Looking around at the hundred or so local farmers, I wished I could take a picture of their interesting faces, lined and worn by their outdoor lives, eyes screwed up as though searching for a lost animal on their land, and their caps — some to the front, some to the side, some even backwards.

The only woman in the building, I sat with these men, up above the auctioneer's stand and the circle in which the animals to be sold were shown, learning how the bidding and dealing was done. I was soon lifting my fingers or nodding my head, but the farmers were always too quick for me. Finally, when I had picked up my courage, I made a successful bid for a pretty little calf which was being driven around the circle below, all the time being hit by a stick. Why do farmers always feel they must carry a stick with which to hit their animals? Cows never will hurry, one of their most attractive characteristics to my mind.

Now the proud owner of a little beauty, hardly a week old, I carried it in my arms to the car boot, where the farmers gathered around me, saying "Ye'll never rear it, it's too young, and the legs are weak." Not a bit worried by their warnings — which I put down to the usual "What could a woman know about such things?" — I hurried home, a matter of five or six miles, to settle the animal in its own warm shed, collecting a bag of the best calf food on the way. It drank a few buckets full, and grew day by day into a splendid animal.

When Noel saw the calf he was really pleased. "Imagine," he said excitedly, "we'll have our own milk in time!" That was a big mistake, an example of how little either of us knew, not our first, nor our last mistake — for it wasn't to grow up to be that sort of cow! Indeed, I'm still unsure of the differences in cows, cattle and heifers. A few weeks later we bought an older animal at the mart, her appearance making it clear to us that she would have milk sometime. 'She' eventually had a calf to our surprise, but there was still no milk for us, the new little calf needing it. I named the mother 'Elsa', and she became like a pet dog. At four o'clock every afternoon I would call her, and Elsa would race up to me at the gate where I was waiting with a basinful of oats.

The day her calf was born I was by myself in the house. Hearing an enormous roar, I ran down through the fields to see what was wrong. Elsa had dropped the poor new-born calf into the river, luckily only a few feet deep. All I could do was to get into the water, lift the calf out, and carry it back to the house, while Elsa walked beside me, continually mooing.

I quickly wrapped the little thing in dry sacks and laid it on plenty of straw, after which it eventually struggled to its feet to be looked after by its mother. On this particular day Noel was at a Labour Party meeting in Dublin, where I phoned the Party leader, Mr Brendan Corish, to ask him to tell Noel the news, so that he'd get home as quickly as he could. I didn't want to lose the little calf, nor indeed its mother. Mr Corish, whenever I met him afterwards, always smilingly asked me how the calf was progressing.

Considering how little we knew about farming, we were quite proud at how we managed our animals, working together in a very organised fashion. Noel understood the ponies better than I did, whereas the smaller animals, calves and piglets, were easier for me. We looked upon the work as a pleasant experience, for we both realised that one would need to be much younger to keep going at such a rate for many years. Meanwhile it was pleasant for our daughters to visit us when they were free, for picnics and walks. In good weather we would harness one of the ponies and take a drive in our lovely old 'back-to-back' trap, a most pleasurable way to travel, sometimes to our nearest town Roundwood, where we could enjoy a drink.

While I was alone in the house, so hidden, I never worried about the possibility of unwelcome visitors. But one morning, when Noel had gone to work in St Brendan's, a farmer called, pulling a horse, and large cart full of turnips for sale. He seemed an ordinary sort of hard-working man, but I felt a little nervous talking to him, his speech being difficult to discern, and one of his big eyes very crooked.

We sometimes ate turnips with potatoes for an evening meal, so I asked the farmer for two or three. However he expected me to take the whole lot, as the vegetables were for animal feed. With a look of disgust he turned his horse and cart and went off muttering.

When living in the hospital lodge, we never bothered to lock the back or front door, nor did we in Djouce. One fine Sunday morning, when we were all together for the day, we decided to have a picnic further up the mountain, where there was a stream, even a little waterfall, in which we could cool ourselves. Before leaving I put a small meal into the oven, so that it would cook slowly and be ready for us when we returned home hungry. On arriving home after a pleasant day in the sun, to my amazement, on opening the oven I found it absolutely empty. How on earth could that have happened? A few weeks went by before we solved the mystery.

From time to time we passed a harmless young man walking on the main road. While not meaning to be unkind, he was what we called 'not the full shilling'. Could he have been the culprit? We guessed the answer was 'Yes' when, one morning, a chocolate cake walked out of my oven while we were far away in the fields, busy with the animals. Though I felt bad about locking our doors from then on, I thought it wise to do so, as this man already looked healthy and well-fed!

We were luckier with the pigs than we were with the toothless sheep and the poor hens, the main reason being because they were properly housed, no home-made concrete block affairs two-feet high, as Noel had constructed in the hospital garden.

Now we had proper sties, with their own gates and troughs. Every Sunday we cleared them out and made them dry with new bedding. We did have one unfortunate episode, though, when one of us forgot to close the gates. Of course the clever animals got out and had a wild morning investigating their surroundings. It so happened that the night before had been extremely stormy, and the land was soaking wet from a heavy rainfall. Meanwhile, the corrugated iron roof of the large shed the ponies sheltered in had fallen down, and while Noel was busy trying to quieten the frightened animals and restore the roof, I was running in all directions trying to collect the pigs, and bring them back to their sties.

As they were enjoying their freedom, I was becoming exhausted. "I'll fill a bucket or two of their favourite food," I decided, "then they'll follow me." This I did, and this they did too: hearing the bucket sound, they raced from all corners to reach the food, knocking me down in their excitement. I didn't just fall on the ground, but through it — for, like long ago on the mountain walk with Noel, when I lost my shoes, I sank into the muddy ground. Helplessly stuck in the mud, with the pigs helping themselves to the food in the buckets, I could only groan, as they licked my face. Noel eventually heard my yells for help, and pulling me up, could not stop laughing at the sight. What a morning that was; both of us were exhausted, and agreed we were beyond such physical effort at our stage of life.

This episode in our lives was ultimately ended by nothing more natural than the weather. Winter came, our third winter on Djouce, covering our fields with snow so thick that food for livestock was dropped by helicopters. All our animals had to be gathered into the large cobbled square at the back of our house, and any who could shelter into the sheds did so.

It must have been the worst winter since 1947, the year our Sue was born, when I could not leave the house for weeks, snowbound. Everything had to be sold and at a loss of course. We were convinced however that this misfortune, sad as it was, was telling us to be sensible, to gather up our belongings and make our final journey, the one we always knew we would, the journey to our cottage in Connemara. And it would not be long now before we did just that.

Our Journey's End

In the early Eighties we finally 'packed it in' and moved to Connemara for good, not feeling the least bit guilty this time. Younger men were entering politics, and it was time to make way for them. We could only hope they would find the answers to the many problems our country faced. Meanwhile, Noel's health, I could see, was deteriorating, though he was not complaining. More than anything else, I wished for him a few years during which he could be himself, have time to read books of his choice, not Dáil reports, and time to take walks by the sea, before either of us felt the gentle touch on the shoulder. For over forty years he had never felt really free — even when sailing, he always knew he had something waiting to be seen to, and so must return to harbour.

Light-hearted, contented, good-humoured, we left the city behind us. By this stage both Ruth and Susan were married. Ruth, who had taken art lessons from the well-known Yann Goulet, and had qualified as a piano teacher from the Royal Irish Academy of Music, had taught these subjects in various schools up until the time of her marriage. Susan meanwhile had worked in the Records Office of the Meath Hospital until her marriage to a doctor, who also worked there, in 1967. Over the coming years we were to become the proud grandparents of four wonderful grandchildren: Nena, Ruth's daughter, and Glyn, Cormac and Ruairi, Susan's three boys.

So here we were at last, in Connemara, and I had a good feeling that we were here to stay. No more house moving. Noel had never been more contented with his surroundings, no limits, the next stop over the seas to New York.

In no time we had a routine: breakfast in bed, the tray laid out the night before, an hour or two talking about the radio news, for whatever was politically interesting still mattered to us. I'd drive then to the local shop for the newspaper, and any basic food we required. How pleasant it was to pass the lake on the way, and admire the swans, such beautiful creatures, or stop to watch a few lazy herons fly by on their secret journey. I'd meet a few of the local ladies in the shop, always cheerful and polite, and with plenty of time to spare, as there is no hurry about life here. We seldom knew the time of day, as none of our clocks kept time, and we'd put the radio on for that information. We would even forget what day of the week it was, finding out only by reading the top of the newspaper.

Whatever the weather, and it was seldom the same two days in succession, Noel would walk down to the sea's edge, passing gentle cows, and noticing any new flower. He'd find a comfortable corner in which to sit and read, to the music of the waves rolling in onto the rocks.

I'd get through my housework, taking my time, and when a meal was almost ready, drive down to collect him, for it was too hilly now for him to walk back. I'd sit, also, enjoying the same sounds, learning the names of the various birds from our new bird book, while the birds themselves patiently sat at the rock edges watching out for their fish-teas.

An occasional trip into Galway had to be taken for special purchases, but after a short time there, we'd feel a great desire to return home where we felt safe and happy just to be together. City noises and concrete paths we had quickly come to dislike.

It is always a pleasure to welcome visitors, and we had many, especially in the summer. In early summer our sunsets were unbelievably beautiful, quite impossible to describe; yet winter, with its blue and grey skies, could be beautiful also, especially when the colours of the clouds reflect in the lake, and all is covered in a fine mist.

As our life passed so swiftly through these last two decades, it was inevitable that, as with all mortals whose bones and brains become less able, our pleasures should become more and more gentle, with music being our greatest. Age steals upon us, unseen like the wind, not noticed unless we look in the mirror.

However, Noel was gradually becoming more frail, unable to fight off a chest infection, and this set-back necessitated a visit to Galway, a reluctant visit to the doctor. A heart problem then forced him to rest in the hospital. When home again, he forced himself to take his afternoon walks, but now using a walking stick. Meanwhile, his appetite for good food, even wine, gradually disappeared.

Still, he would talk over the past, remembering in detail every good thing which had happened to him: for despite much unhappiness and difficulties, he really had had a charmed life. By the kindness of the Chance family he had been able to go to Trinity and become a doctor; by chance of a different kind he became a politician, and by the greatest chance of all, we had happily married. Not that it was all behind him yet. One of the most exciting events he liked to talk about was the day Trinity honoured him with a Fellowship in 1994, and finally, a truly memorable evening in 1995 when he spoke from the pulpit in St Patrick's Cathedral, the same pulpit Jonathan Swift had used, to speak to the crowd of people concerned with Aids, in the hope of helping them. He never became bitter either about how the Labour Party or the Church had treated him. It was I who felt quite angry at times, feeling that he was wasted in politics.

The End Approaches, 1997

I could see the grim reaper coming, for Noel's movements were becoming slower, and he looked more frail day by day. Sitting in his chair in silence, most unusual for him, he watched my every movement, as though I would disappear. Much as I wished to, I would not mention that he ought to have a visit from the doctor, for I knew I would have no success, that I would have to wait for him to suggest it himself.

This he did one morning in May 1997, quietly asking me did I think he should have the doctor's advice, which greatly relieved me, for I was really worried for him. Since our first days together, so long ago, we had often spoken of how one would cope without the other, and wondered how? Now I had to summon all the courage I possessed, to phone for a ambulance, to speak with the doctor. I thought I had steeled my heart for the final parting, but I was not ready. For all our years together, sixty-two in all, it made no difference. I was not ready, indeed forlorn, and I wondered would I ever again be the person I had become since our first meeting, when I was just sixteen. A bird with a broken wing cannot fly.

The End Comes

As he lay in his hospital bed for his last two days, I spoke soothingly to him, but he did not hear me. His once beautiful brown eyes were closed, his once clear intelligent speech was but a jumbled murmur. Alone with him, holding his hands, thin and cold, hands which had worked so hard, I listened to his weakening heartbeats. I sat there, transfixed, becoming colder and colder, as he was. I felt I was in a horrible dream, unable to believe what was happening.

Why would I wish to live without him, and his gentle loving ways? Who now would untie my shoelaces, put my slippers on, share everything with me? His first task in the morning was to feed the garden birds, calling out to them to leave the shelter of the warm thatch. His last request, slowly whispered, was to not forget to feed the birds.

Semi-conscious, I at last got the strength to rise from the chair, give him my good-bye kiss upon his white forehead, and reluctantly leave him to face the world outside, helped by the kind doctor.

It is over now. His hands no longer reach out to mine as they did when, sitting by the turf fire in the evenings, we would listen to our favourite music. His goodnight smile and kiss upon my head are but memories. Yet I hear his gentle voice still, talk with him still. I feel his presence, but there is no consolation. It would probably surprise some people to know that Noel had a most loving, romantic side to his character. Serious and reserved in his work, at home he was quite different, enjoying domestic life and the company of our daughters with a deep quiet pride. Their young families gave him a loving interest, a joy which he had missed in his own family. How we all miss him.

Even with the help of the many kind people who tried to comfort me with letters, as well as the understanding journalists, I will never again be able to face life with the joy in my heart which had kept me strong and brave for so many hard years. Our life had been a stormy passage, made happy by a love which "passed all understanding".

He lies in the clean sandy soil by the Atlantic shore, where he liked to sit every afternoon, seagulls and screaming curlews flying above him. In time, the tiny wild flowers there will grow to cover him in nature's beauty, flowers which he would sometimes bring home in a bouquet, three or four only, and present them to me, as though they were orchids.